FRANCIS FRITH'S

VALE OF EVESHAM

PHOTOGRAPHIC MEMORIES

JULIE ROYLE was born in Cheshire and grew up there and in Northumbria. She studied history at the University of Exeter. She now lives near Worcester, in a small country cottage with a large unruly garden, and works as a freelance photographer and writer specialising in landscape, wildlife, travel, conservation, environmental issues and local history.

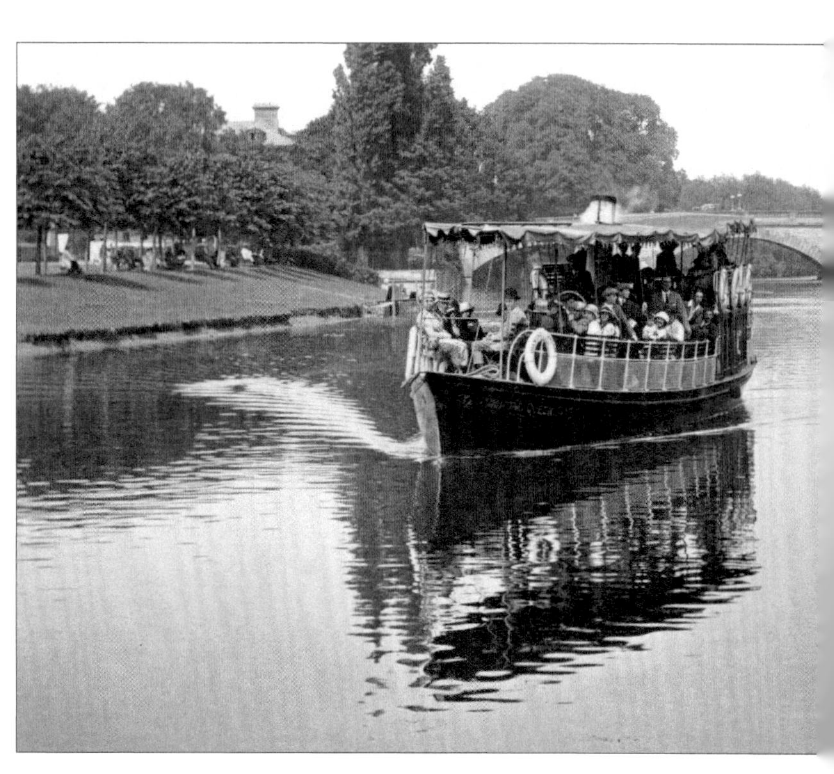

FRANCIS FRITH'S
PHOTOGRAPHIC MEMORIES

VALE OF EVESHAM

PHOTOGRAPHIC MEMORIES

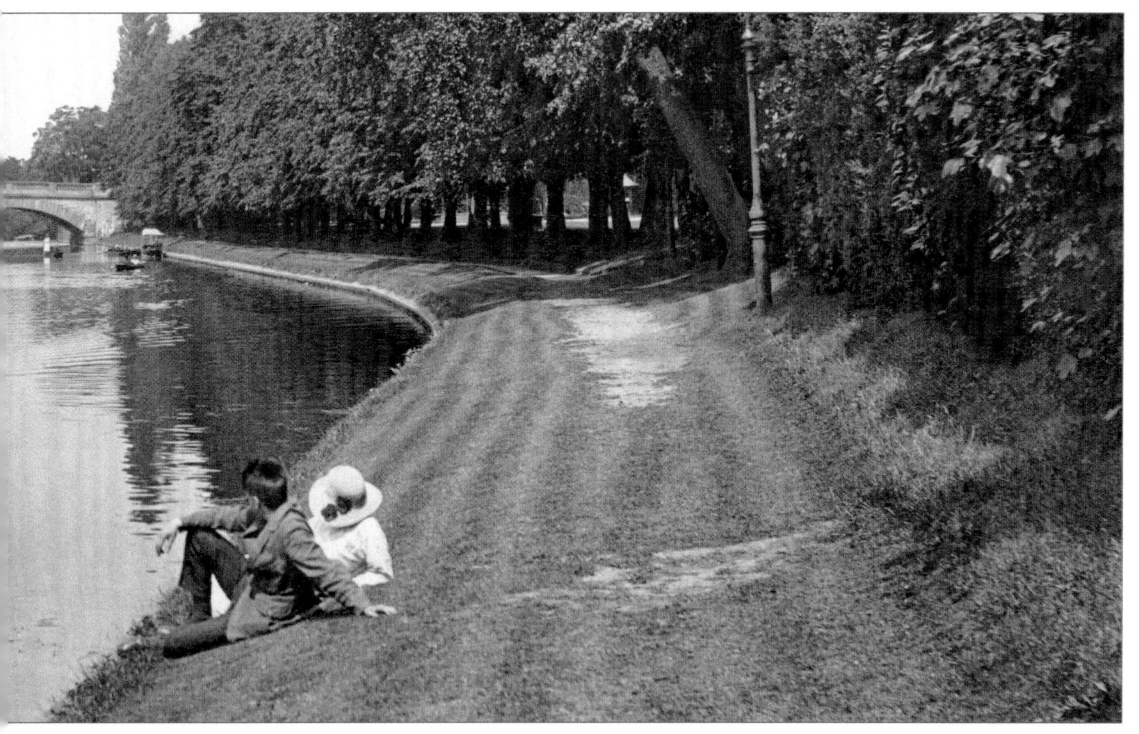

JULIE ROYLE

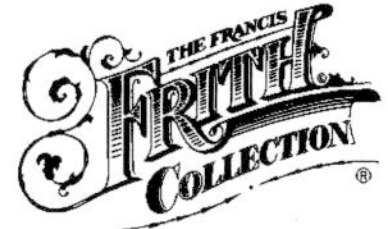

First published in paperback in the United Kingdom in 2006 by
The Francis Frith Collection®

ISBN 10: 1-84589-147-3   ISBN 13: 978-1-84589-147-3

British Library Cataloguing in Publication Data

Vale of Evesham - Photographic Memories
Julie Royle

The Francis Frith Collection
Frith's Barn, Teffont,
Salisbury, Wiltshire SP3 5QP
Tel: +44 (0) 1722 716 376
Email: info@francisfrith.co.uk
www.francisfrith.com

Printed and bound in Great Britain

Front Cover: **EVESHAM,** *Bridge Street 1892* 31106t
Frontispiece: **EVESHAM,** *The River and the Bridge 1922* 72428

The colour-tinting is for illustrative purposes only, and is not intended to be historically accurate

Aerial photographs reproduced under licence from Simmons Aerofilms Limited.
Historical Ordnance Survey maps reproduced under licence from Homecheck.co.uk
Every attempt has been made to contact copyright holders of illustrative material.
We will be happy to give full acknowledgement in future editions for any items not credited.
Any information should be directed to The Francis Frith Collection.

AS WITH ANY HISTORICAL DATABASE THE FRITH ARCHIVE IS CONSTANTLY BEING
CORRECTED AND IMPROVED AND THE PUBLISHERS WOULD WELCOME INFORMATION
ON OMISSIONS OR INACCURACIES

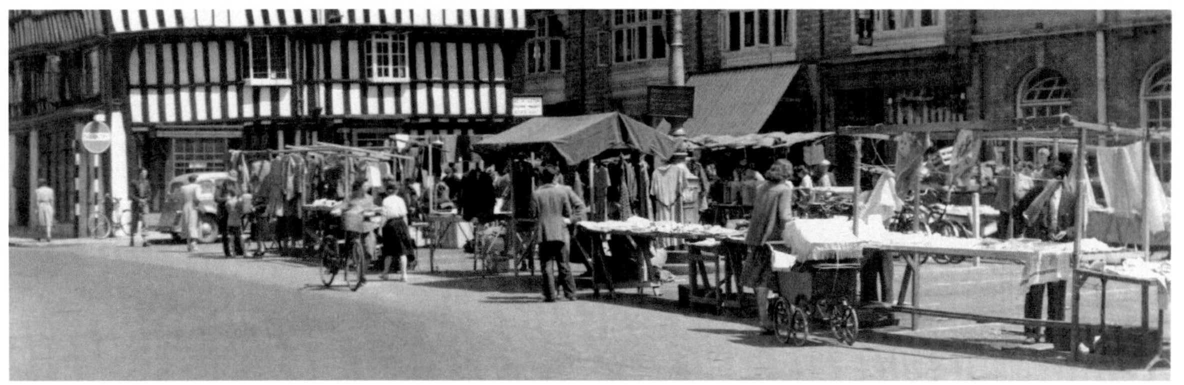

CONTENTS

FRANCIS FRITH: VICTORIAN PIONEER   7

VALE OF EVESHAM - AN INTRODUCTION   10

REMINDERS OF EVESHAM ABBEY   15

MARKET PLACE, HIGH STREET AND VINE STREET   24

EVESHAM ORDNANCE SURVEY MAP   38

BRIDGE STREET, ABBEY PARK AND THE RIVER AVON   40

EVESHAM FROM THE AIR   48

WORCESTERSHIRE COUNTY MAP   58

DOWNSTREAM FROM EVESHAM   60

UPSTREAM FROM EVESHAM   80

INDEX   89

Free Mounted Print Voucher   93

FRANCIS FRITH
VICTORIAN PIONEER

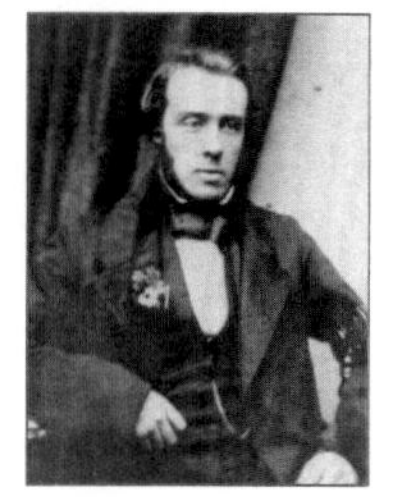

FRANCIS FRITH, founder of the world-famous photographic archive, was a complex and multi-talented man. A devout Quaker and a highly successful Victorian businessman, he was philosophical by nature and pioneering in outlook.

By 1855 he had already established a wholesale grocery business in Liverpool, and sold it for the astonishing sum of £200,000, which is the equivalent today of over £15,000,000. Now a very rich man, he was able to indulge his passion for travel. As a child he had pored over travel books written by early explorers, and his fancy and imagination had been stirred by family holidays to the sublime mountain regions of Wales and Scotland. 'What lands of spirit-stirring and enriching scenes and places!' he had written. He was to return to these scenes of grandeur in later years to 'recapture the thousands of vivid and tender memories', but with a different purpose. Now in his thirties, and captivated by the new science of photography, Frith set out on a series of pioneering journeys up the Nile and to the Near East that occupied him from 1856 until 1860.

INTRIGUE AND EXPLORATION

These far-flung journeys were packed with intrigue and adventure. In his life story, written when he was sixty-three, Frith tells of being held captive by bandits, and of fighting 'an awful midnight battle to the very point of surrender with a deadly pack of hungry, wild dogs'. Wearing flowing Arab costume, Frith arrived at Akaba by camel sixty years before Lawrence of Arabia, where he encountered 'desert princes and rival sheikhs, blazing with jewel-hilted swords'.

He was the first photographer to venture beyond the sixth cataract of the Nile. Africa was still the mysterious 'Dark Continent', and Stanley and Livingstone's historic meeting was a decade into the future. The conditions for picture taking confound belief. He laboured for hours in his wicker dark-room in the sweltering heat of the desert, while the volatile chemicals fizzed dangerously in their trays. Back in London he exhibited his photographs and was 'rapturously cheered' by members of the Royal Society. His reputation as a photographer was made overnight.

VENTURE OF A LIFE-TIME

Characteristically, Frith quickly spotted the opportunity to create a new business as a specialist publisher of photographs. He lived

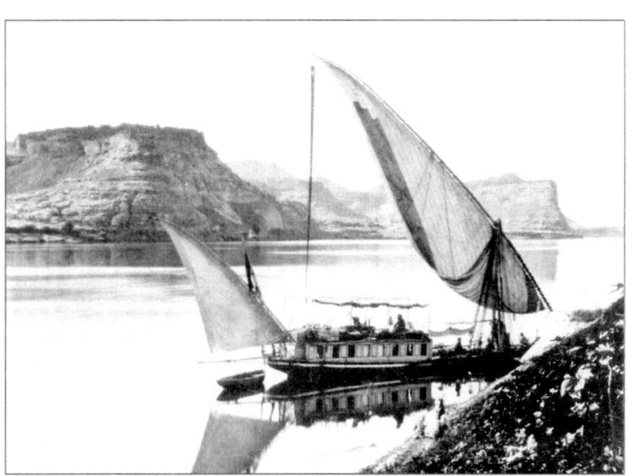

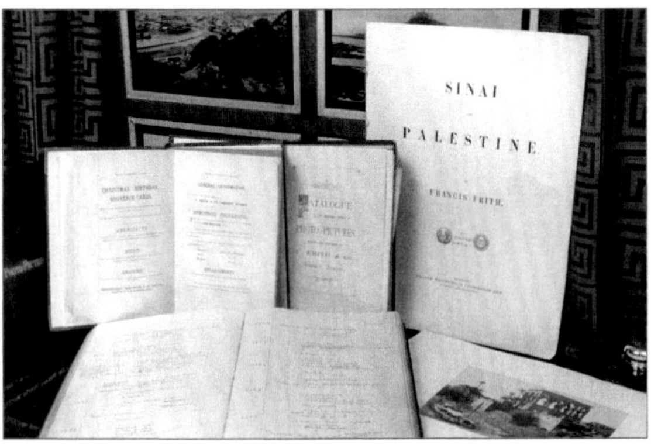

in an era of immense and sometimes violent change. For the poor in the early part of Victoria's reign work was exhausting and the hours long, and people had precious little free time to enjoy themselves. Most had no transport other than a cart or gig at their disposal, and rarely travelled far beyond the boundaries of their own town or village. However, by the 1870s the railways had threaded their way across the country, and Bank Holidays and half-day Saturdays had been made obligatory by Act of Parliament. All of a sudden the working man and his family were able to enjoy days out and see a little more of the world.

With typical business acumen, Francis Frith foresaw that these new tourists would enjoy having souvenirs to commemorate their days out. In 1860 he married Mary Ann Rosling and set out on a new career: his aim was to photograph every city, town and village in Britain. For the next thirty years he travelled the country by train and by pony and trap, producing fine photographs of seaside resorts and beauty spots that were keenly bought by millions of Victorians. These prints were painstakingly pasted into family albums and pored over during the dark nights of winter, rekindling precious memories of summer excursions.

THE RISE OF FRITH & CO

Frith's studio was soon supplying retail shops all over the country. To meet the demand he gathered about him a small team of photographers, and published the work of independent artist-photographers of the calibre of Roger Fenton and Francis Bedford. In order to gain some understanding of the scale of Frith's business one only has to look at the catalogue issued by Frith & Co in 1886: it runs to some 670 pages, listing not only many thousands of views of the British Isles but also many photographs of most European countries, and China, Japan, the USA and Canada - note the sample page shown on page 9 from the hand-written Frith & Co ledgers recording the pictures. By 1890 Frith had created the greatest specialist photographic publishing company in the world, with over 2,000 sales outlets - more than the combined number that Boots and WH Smith have today! The picture on the next page shows the Frith & Co display board at Ingleton in the Yorkshire Dales (left of window). Beautifully constructed with a mahogany frame and gilt inserts, it could display up to a dozen local scenes.

POSTCARD BONANZA

The ever-popular holiday postcard we know today took many years to develop. In 1870 the Post Office issued the first plain cards, with a pre-printed stamp on one face. In 1894 they allowed other publishers' cards to be sent through the mail with an attached adhesive halfpenny stamp. Demand grew rapidly, and in 1895 a new size of postcard was permitted called the court card, but there was little room for illustration. In 1899, a year after Frith's death, a new card measuring 5.5 x 3.5 inches became the standard format, but it was not until 1902 that the divided back came into being, so that the address and message could be on one face and a full-size illustration on the other. Frith & Co were in the vanguard of postcard development: Frith's sons Eustace and Cyril continued their father's monumental task, expanding the number of views offered to the public and recording more and more places

5	... College, View from the garden
6	St Catherine's College
7	Senate House & Library
8	
9	Gerrard Hostel Bridge
30	Geological Museum
1	Addenbrooke's Hospital
2	St Mary's Church
3	Fitzwilliam Museum, Pitt Press &c
4	
5	Buxton, The Crescent
6	The Colonnade
7	Public Gardens
8	
9	Haddon Hall, View from the Terrace
40	Miller's Dale.

in Britain, as the coasts and countryside were opened up to mass travel.

Francis Frith had died in 1898 at his villa in Cannes, his great project still growing. The archive he created continued in business for another seventy years. By 1970 it contained over a third of a million pictures showing 7,000 British towns and villages.

FRANCIS FRITH'S LEGACY

Frith's legacy to us today is of immense significance and value, for the magnificent archive of evocative photographs he created provides a unique record of change in the cities, towns and villages throughout Britain over a century and more. Frith and his fellow studio photographers revisited locations many times down the years to update their views, compiling for us an enthralling and colourful pageant of British life and character.

We are fortunate that Frith was dedicated to recording the minutiae of everyday life, for it is this sheer wealth of visual data, the painstaking chronicle of changes in dress, transport, street layouts, buildings, housing, engineering and landscape that captivates us so much today. His remarkable images offer us a powerful link with the past and with the lives of our ancestors.

THE VALUE OF THE ARCHIVE TODAY

Computers have now made it possible for Frith's many thousands of images to be accessed almost instantly. Frith's images are increasingly used as visual resources, by social historians, by researchers into genealogy and ancestry, by architects and town planners, and by teachers involved in local history projects.

In addition, the archive offers every one of us an opportunity to examine the places where we and our families have lived and worked down the years. Highly successful in Frith's own era, the archive is now, a century and more on, entering a new phase of popularity. Historians consider the Francis Frith Collection to be of prime national importance. It is the only archive of its kind remaining in private ownership. Francis Frith's archive is now housed in an historic timber barn in the beautiful village of Teffont in Wiltshire. Its founder would not recognize the archive office as it is today. In place of the many thousands of dusty boxes containing glass plate negatives and an all-pervading odour of photographic chemicals, there are now ranks of computer screens. He would be amazed to watch his images travelling round the world at unimaginable speeds through internet lines.

The archive's future is both bright and exciting. Francis Frith, with his unshakeable belief in making photographs available to the greatest number of people, would undoubtedly approve of what is being done today with his lifetime's work. His photographs depicting our shared past are now bringing pleasure and enlightenment to millions around the world a century and more after his death.

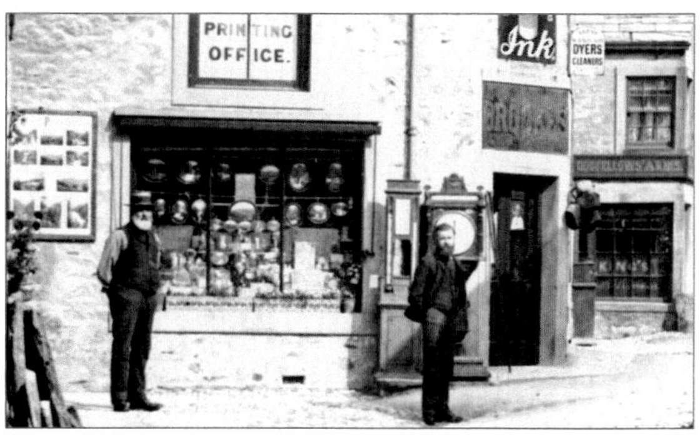

VALE OF EVESHAM
AN INTRODUCTION

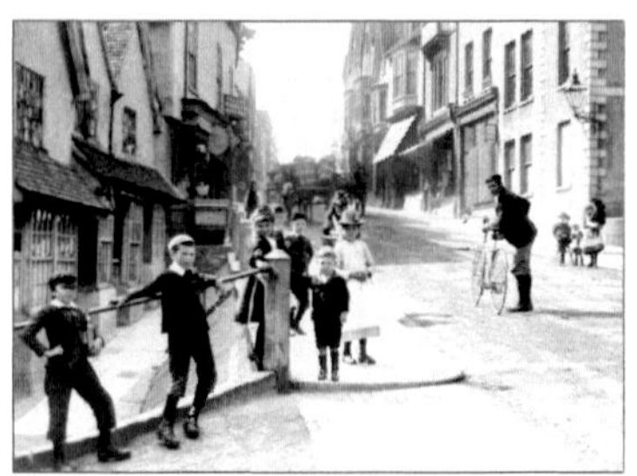

THE MARKET TOWN of Evesham is situated in a loop of the River Avon, which encloses it on three sides. It lies at the centre of the Vale of Evesham, a low-lying area of country whose limits are not sharply defined. Daniel Defoe, writing c1725, described it as 'that fruitful and plentiful country which was call'd the Vale Of Esham, which runs all along the banks of The Avon, from Tewksbury to Pershore, and so to Stratford upon Avon, and in the south part of Warwickshire ...' Nowadays it is generally considered to cover a slightly smaller area than that. Few people consider it extends as far as Stratford, for example, nor even quite so far as Tewkesbury. Essentially, it belongs to Worcestershire.

Archaeological finds indicate that semi-nomadic people were present in the vale in the Stone Age, and there seems to have been

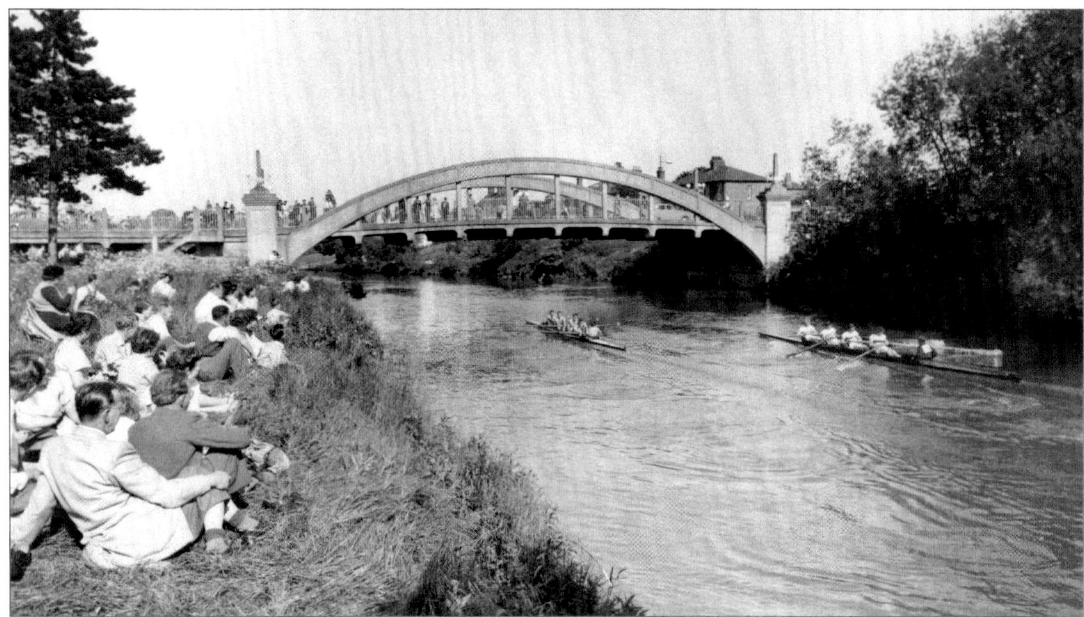

EVESHAM, *The River and the Bridge c1955* E44079

continuous settlement ever since. However, Evesham's story really begins cAD700 with the legend of a swineherd called Eoves who saw a vision of the Virgin Mary. When this was reported to Bishop (later Saint) Egwin of Worcester, the bishop went to the same spot and saw a similar vision in which the Virgin told him to build a church. Egwin was given land by King Ethelred of Mercia and he built a monastic church, which was completed in AD714 and dedicated to the Virgin Mary. Egwin resigned as bishop and became its first abbot.

Egwin's abbey was rebuilt, improved or enlarged by almost every subsequent abbot and became one of England's greatest Benedictine monasteries. The abbey church was the size of Gloucester Cathedral, and the monks owned land in several counties. A small town began to develop alongside the abbey, and the monks took steps to help it on its way. In 1055 Edward the Confessor granted it the right to hold a market, confirming that Evesham was growing into an important trading centre.

Politically, Evesham's greatest moment came in 1265 during the Barons' War, which stemmed from the sheer incompetence of Henry III. His barons so despised him that they briefly abandoned their own squabbles and banded together under the leadership of Simon de Montfort, Earl of Leicester, with the aim of forcing the king to accept limitations to his power. In January 1265, with the king a prisoner, Leicester summoned representatives from the shires to a great assembly in London. In the eyes of many historians this was a crucial milestone on the long road to democracy, and Leicester is sometimes referred to as the Father of the English Parliament. However, in August 1265,

at the Battle of Evesham, the Royalist army, commanded by Prince Edward, won a great victory. Leicester was among the 4,000 men who were slaughtered in the battle. Royal power was strengthened as a result of the Battle of Evesham, but Leicester had at least laid the foundations for a limited form of parliamentary representation. His mutilated remains were collected from the battlefield and buried by the monks before the high altar of Evesham Abbey. A memorial stone now marks the putative spot.

Evesham Abbey reached the zenith of its prosperity around 1230, but continued hugely wealthy until it was dissolved by Henry VIII in 1539. The bell tower was purchased for the town and the almonry was granted to Abbot Hawford, but the other monastic buildings were sold to Sir Philip Hoby who plundered them for building stone. So thoroughly did he quarry the site that in 1540 John Leland described it as 'a mere heap of rubbish'. Evesham, however, gradually recovered from the loss of the abbey and began to thrive again. By the 1630s it was a wealthy town, at the centre of a hugely productive agricultural area.

Agriculture has always been important in the vale, which has particularly been associated with fruit growing and market gardening. It was probably the monks who first established the tradition of fruit growing, and the fertile soils made the vale ideal for the task. However, the chief pioneer seems to have been a Genoese named Francisco Bernadi, who settled in the area in the 1650s and set to work to reclaim the rather neglected monastic lands, using new technologies and scientific knowledge to increase yields. He established quite a reputation and attracted a number of local imitators, so that the area gradually became one of the foremost in the country for fruit and vegetable production.

A fact that is often overlooked is that the vale was also a leader in other forms of agriculture. In 1585 William Camden wrote that it yielded 'the best corn abundantly', and Daniel Defoe described it c1725 as 'most pleasant corn country, especially remarkable for the goodness of the air, and fertility of the soil.' William Cobbett, c1830, surveyed the vales of the Severn and the Avon from Bredon Hill, concluding that 'nine-tenths of the land in these extensive vales appears to me to be pasture, and it is pasture of the richest kind.'

There were other industries too, of course: everything from tanning to parchment making, and Defoe wrote that Evesham is 'famous for a great manufacture of stockings'. But agriculture remained pre-eminent.

All this produce was not just for local consumption, and here the Avon came into its own. In 1636, William Sandys of Fladbury Mill was granted a royal charter to improve the navigation. He built locks and weirs between Tewkesbury and Stratford, and by 1665 the Avon had become a major commercial highway. As Defoe wrote, 'the navigation of this river Avon is an exceeding advantage to all this part of the country, and also to the commerce of the city of Bristol.' At its peak in the 1750s there were about 400 barges plying the Avon. There were extensive wharves and warehouses by Evesham Bridge, and each riverside village had its own wharf.

The coming of the railways hit the river trade hard, but gave a huge boost to trade in general. By 1864 Evesham had two lines and two stations, and many vale villages had stations too. Produce could now be transported all over the country at high speed, which was particularly useful for perishables such as fruit and vegetables.

Britain suffered an agricultural depression in the 1870s, but the vale seemed immune. It was helped by the expansion of London - as the capital consumed Middlesex, so Middlesex nurserymen sold up and moved away. Attracted by its reputation, many went to the Vale of Evesham, taking new ideas and new crops with them. James Myatt experimented with cabbages, sprouts and leeks, improving the varieties to suit the local conditions, and also pioneered strawberry growing in the 1870s. Market gardeners from Italy and the Netherlands also moved into the vale, bringing their own ideas and expertise. In 1884 Evesham produced its first tomatoes. In 1905 a group of Evesham market gardeners visited France on a fact-finding tour and subsequently introduced 'French gardening' to the vale. This involved the use of frames or cloches to force early produce, which could then be sold at a premium. But whatever innovations were made, the continuing expansion was mainly brought about by the sheer hard work of a host of smallholders. They did have some advantage over competitors elsewhere, thanks to something known as the Evesham Custom, an ancient customary law which gave the tenant a certain security of tenure as long as he paid his rent, made improvements, practised good management and maximised his crop. In 1908 the Small Holdings and Allotments Act further strengthened the tenants' position. Though the smallholders' plots really were small, that was not necessarily a disadvantage. On a small plot every inch must be used efficiently, and that is exactly what happened. Nothing was wasted, and the vale's productivity owed even more to the industry and efficiency of the smallholders than to its famed fertility.

The growers' success also stimulated other industries. By the early 20th century, Evesham had canning, processing and jam factories, providing even more employment for local residents. Seasonal labour was important too, and harvest time would see an influx of pickers, mostly from industrial areas such as the Black Country, who were happy to spend their holidays from the factories working in the fields.

It is a sad fact that nothing lasts for ever, and the vale has not been immune to modern economic realities. Since the Second World War, the increasing importation of fruit and vegetables from abroad has resulted in a decline in market gardening in the vale. Much of the land is now given over to sheep, or to arable crops. Colour in the landscape is now more often provided by the garish yellow of oil-seed rape than by delicate pink or white blossom. One has only to look at the reduction in hedges to see that many former smallholdings have been amalgamated into large farms. Orchards have been grubbed up, glasshouses and polytunnels have multiplied, and nearly everything is mechanised. A Tesco superstore now stands where Smedleys had a jam factory, next to the goods yard where produce waited to be loaded onto trains. But even today there are surviving smallholders with only a few acres, though they now sell much of their produce from roadside stalls and farm shops, mainly to tourists. Asparagus is particularly popular, with the vale reputedly growing the best in the world. The seasonal workers still come, but in smaller numbers and now mostly from eastern Europe.

Evesham has grown in size, with its fair share of suburban estates, but it is still a country town with a close relationship to the rural life of the vale. Computers may be manufactured in

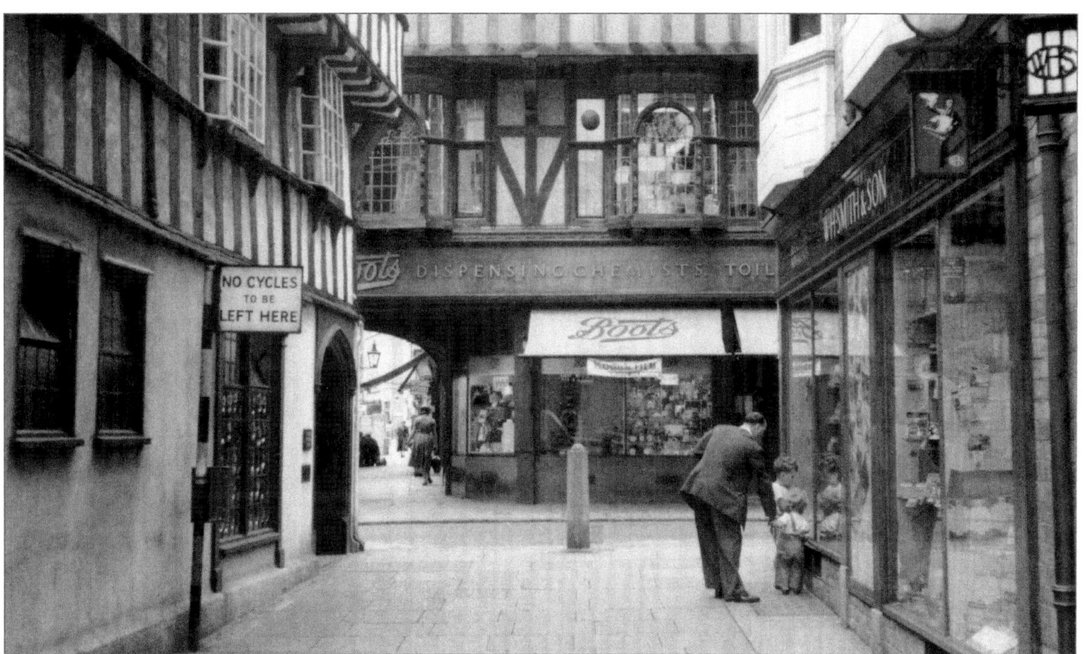

EVESHAM, *Booth Hall c1965* E44100

Evesham today, but crops still grow beside Abbey Road, and orchards still bloom next to Tesco. Glasshouses produce everything from tomatoes to summer bedding plants, and asparagus is still widely grown. Increasingly, Evesham is now a centre for tourism, but even that is partly related to flowers, fruit and vegetables. A Blossom Trail, for instance, is heavily promoted, with visitors encouraged to tour the country lanes during those few weeks when the orchards bloom. Visitors are also attracted to an annual asparagus festival, with an auction at the picturesque Fleece Inn, Bretforton. The pretty village of Cropthorne holds an annual 'Walkabout' when the villagers throw their gardens open to the public, who come in their thousands. Other visitors come to walk or cycle in the Cotswolds, which rise alluringly from the edge of the vale, or along the banks of the Avon. Those who enjoy boats are also increasingly drawn to the Avon. Some come for the regattas and festivals, while others arrive in their own narrowboats or cruisers. Though the navigation decayed after the advent of the railways, it has been restored, with much of the work done by volunteers. In 1950 the Lower Avon Navigation Trust was formed, and by 1962 it had restored the navigation between Tewkesbury and Evesham. By 1974, the Upper Avon Navigation Trust had completed the work to Stratford.

Evesham makes a good base for resident and tourist alike. It remains small enough to be pleasant, and it was fortunate enough to escape some of the worst architectural excesses of the 1950s-70s. The basic layout of the centre is relatively unchanged since the days of the monks, and one has only to raise one's eyes above the brash modern fascias at street level to see that many beautiful 17th-, 18th- and 19th-century buildings survive. In fact, many are much older, but acquired smart new façades in times of prosperity, mainly during the Georgian period. Just a few paces from the bustle of Bridge Street one can step through Abbot Reginald's Gateway into the peace of Abbey Park, with its splendid monastic remains and its access to the River Avon. Over 1,300 years after Egwin founded what was to become one of England's wealthiest abbeys, the town named after Eoves the swineherd remains a lively, attractive, prosperous place with much to offer.

REMINDERS OF EVESHAM ABBEY

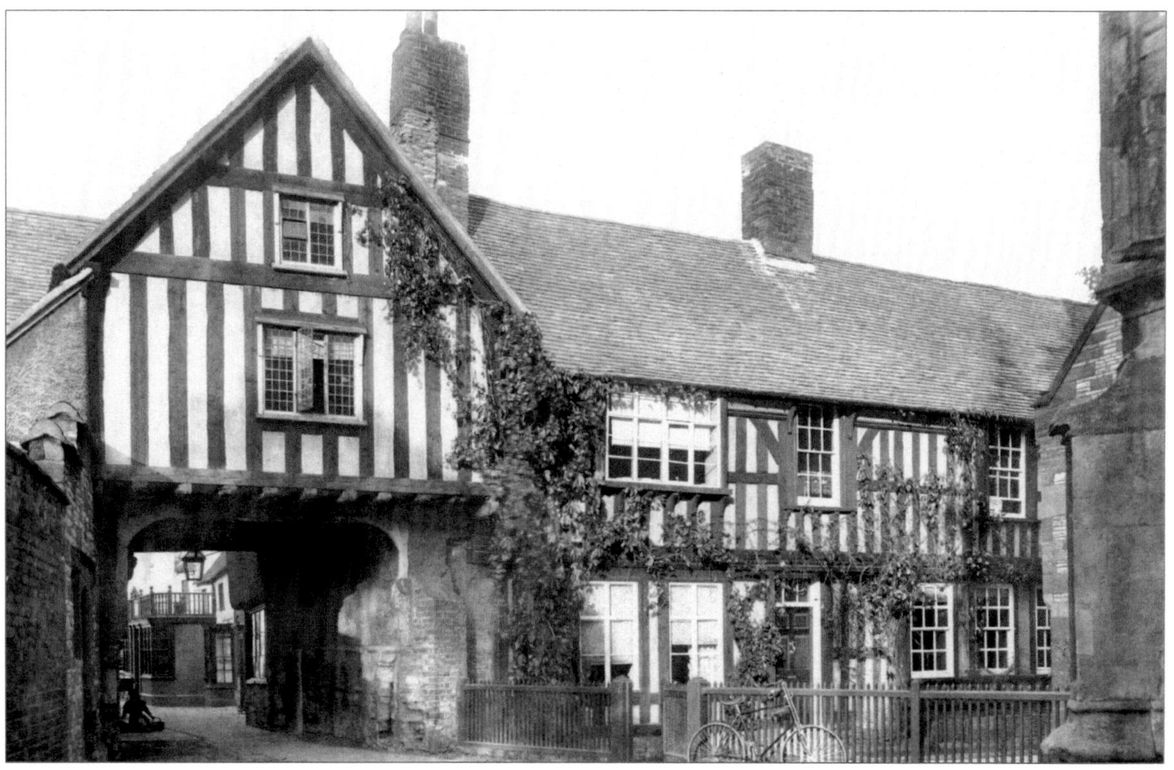

ABBOT REGINALD'S GATEWAY *1895* 36962

This gateway linking the abbey precinct with Market Place (see also 31104 and E44101, pages 24 and 25) was built c1130 by Reginald of Gloucester, who was Abbot of Evesham from 1122 to 1149. The timber-framed structure above it was built later. To the right is 15th-century Church House, which used to be the vicarage. All Saints' Church is just visible on the right-hand edge of the photograph.

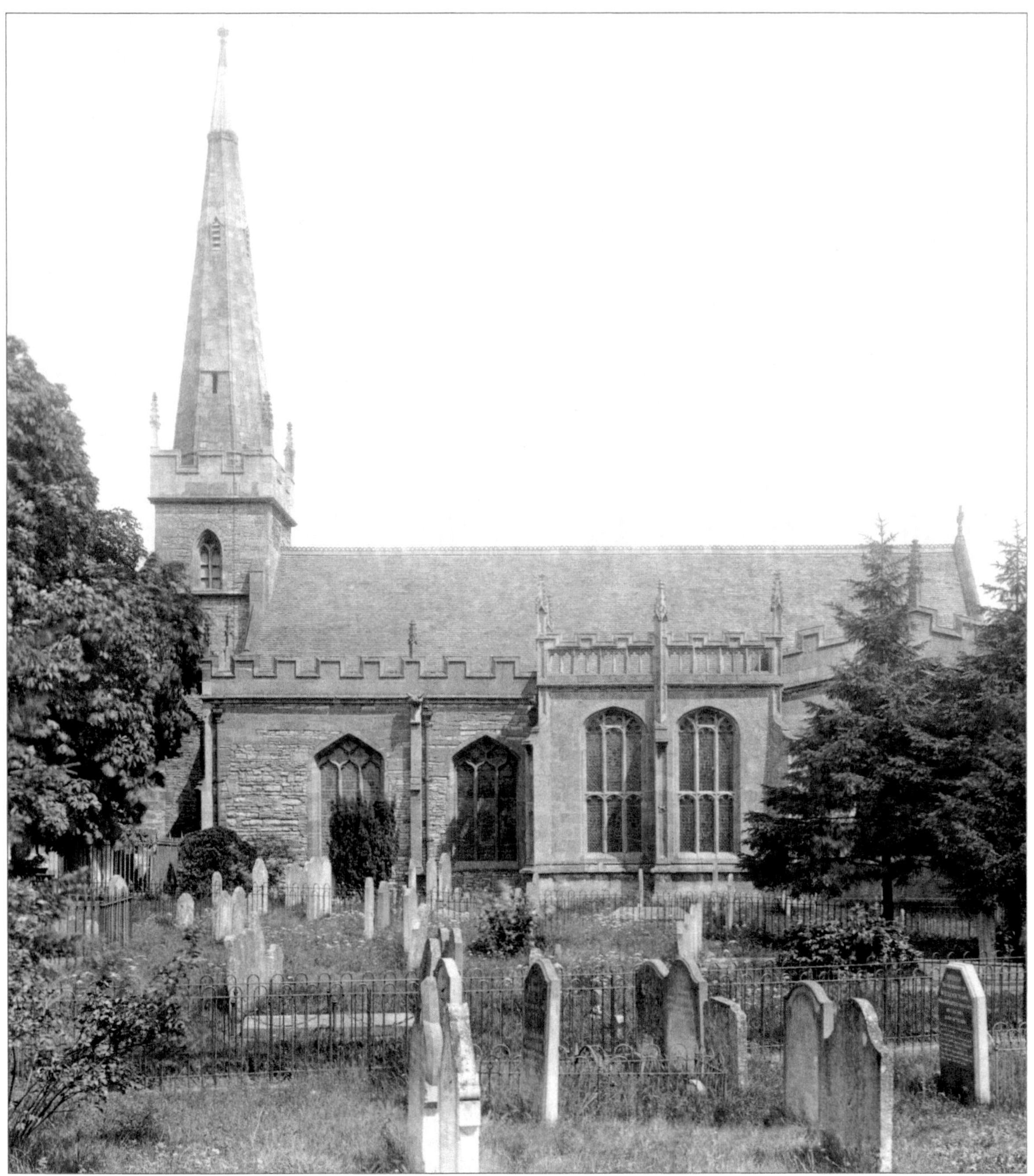

ALL SAINTS' CHURCH *1901* 47314

This is the parish church, which has been in continuous use since it was built by the abbey for the use of the townsfolk in the late 12th century. The Perpendicular extension visible here is the Lichfield Chapel, built by Prior Clement Lichfield in the early 16th century. He later became Abbot Lichfield and was buried in the chapel in 1546.

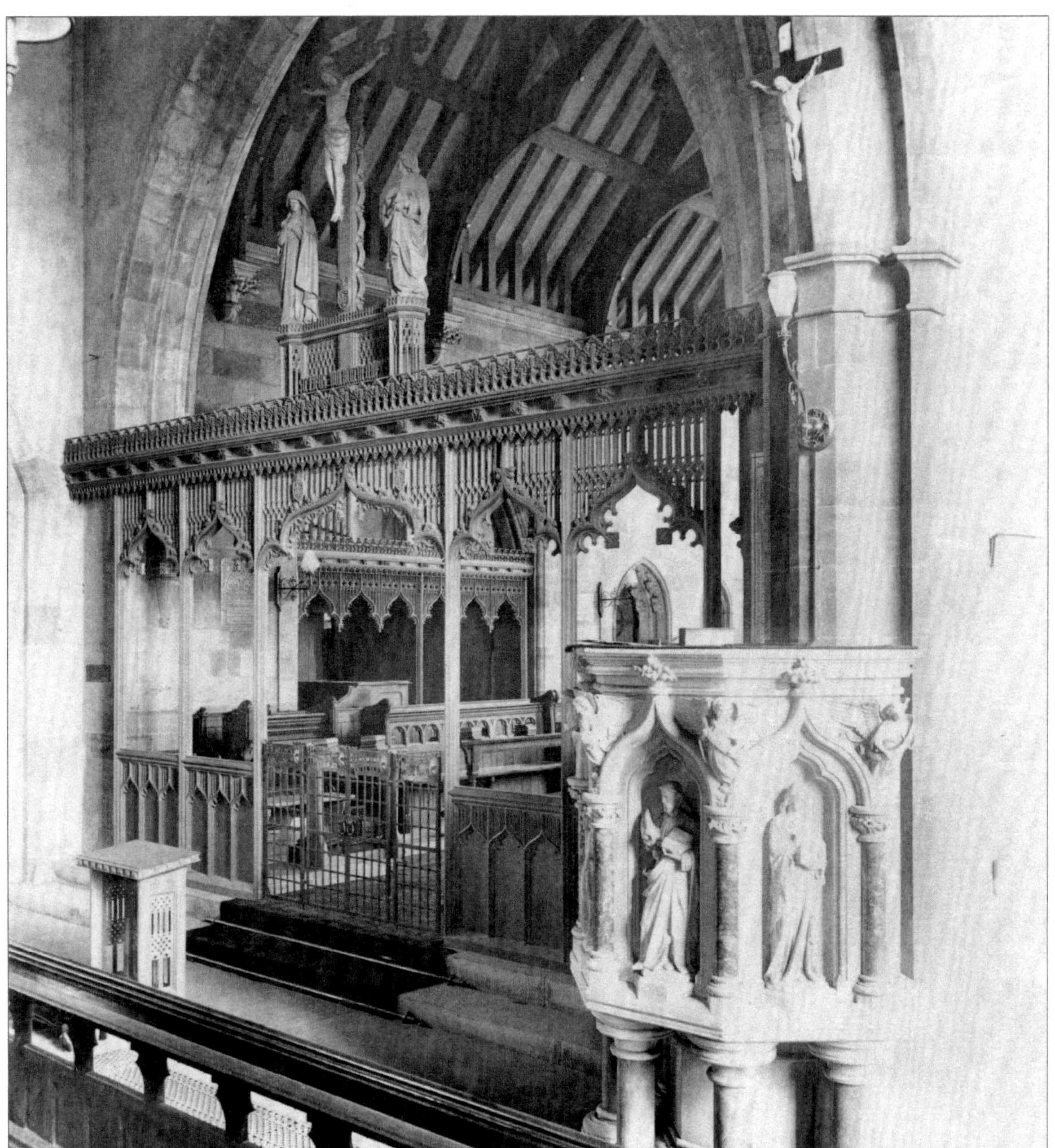

ALL SAINTS' CHURCH, *The Interior 1910* 62351

Though originally built in the 12th century, the church owes much of its present appearance to rebuilding works in the 1870s. This view shows a glimpse of the chancel (built 1875) from the nave. The rood screen dividing the two was carved by local craftsmen Charles and Horace Salmon in 1905 in the Decorated style. The crucifix above the screen is from Oberammergau, but the figures flanking it, of the Virgin Mary and St John, were made in Worcester in 1905 by Richard Haughton. The chancel gates were completed in 1910 in the style of the Arts and Crafts movement.

ST LAWRENCE'S CHURCH *1895* 36964

St Lawrence's stands next to All Saints', but nobody knows why the monks built two adjacent churches. St Lawrence's fell into ruin in the 18th century and underwent a major restoration by the architect Harvey Eginton in 1836-37. On the south side is a chapel dedicated to St Clement, built by Clement Lichfield c1510. It has a superb fan-vaulted roof with fine carving.

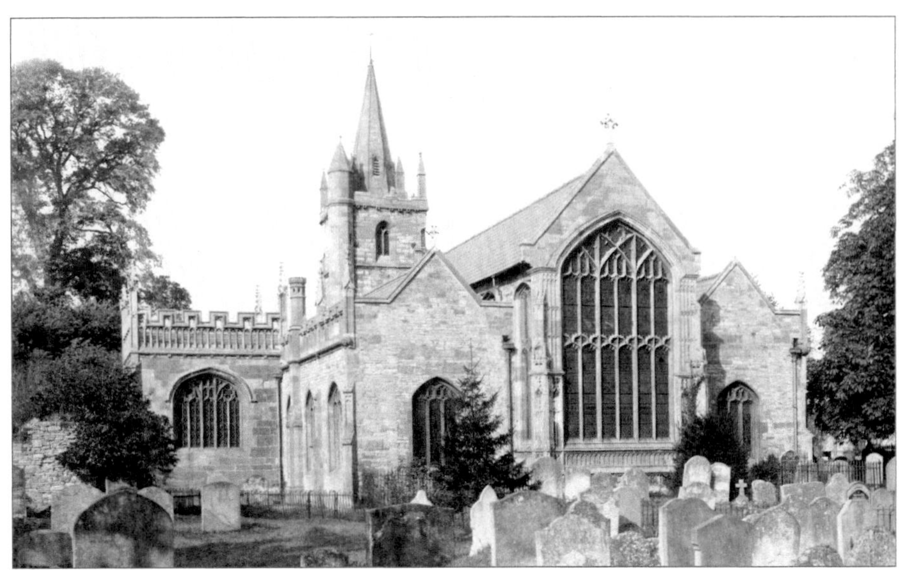

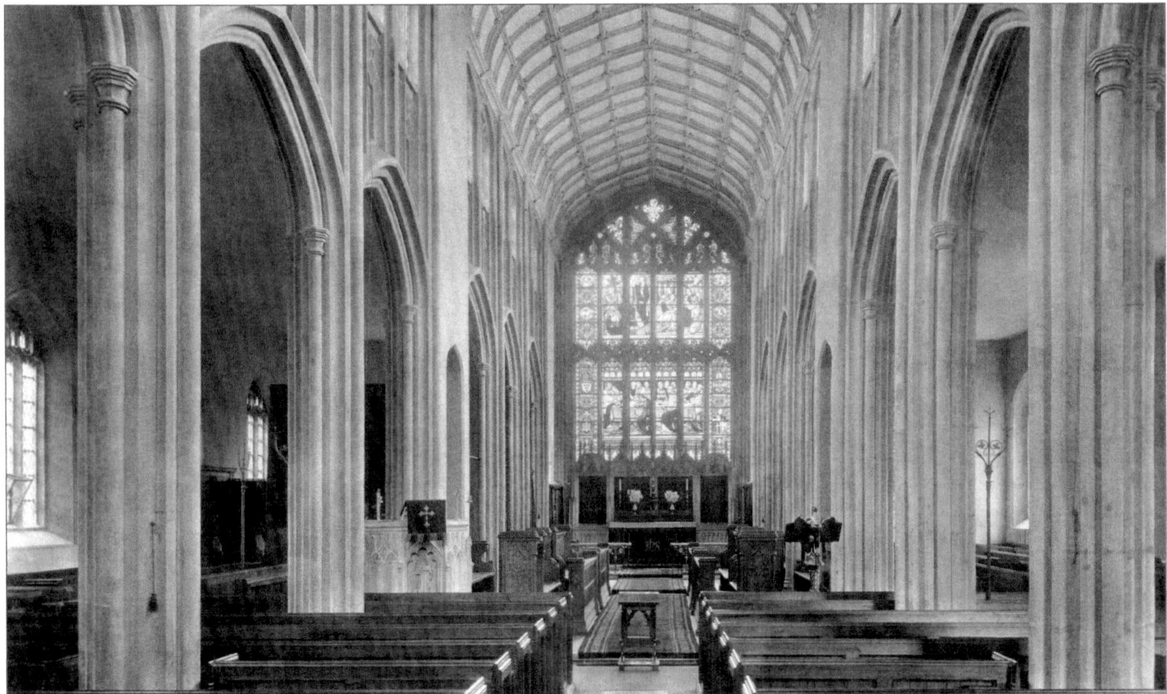

ST LAWRENCE'S CHURCH, *The Interior 1901* 47318

The light and spacious feel of St Lawrence's interior remains unaltered today. No longer used for worship, the church was declared redundant in 1978 and vested in the Churches Conservation Trust which has carried out a restoration programme. St Lawrence's is open daily and occasional services are held - for instance, the service held on St Lawrence's Day (10 August) each year.

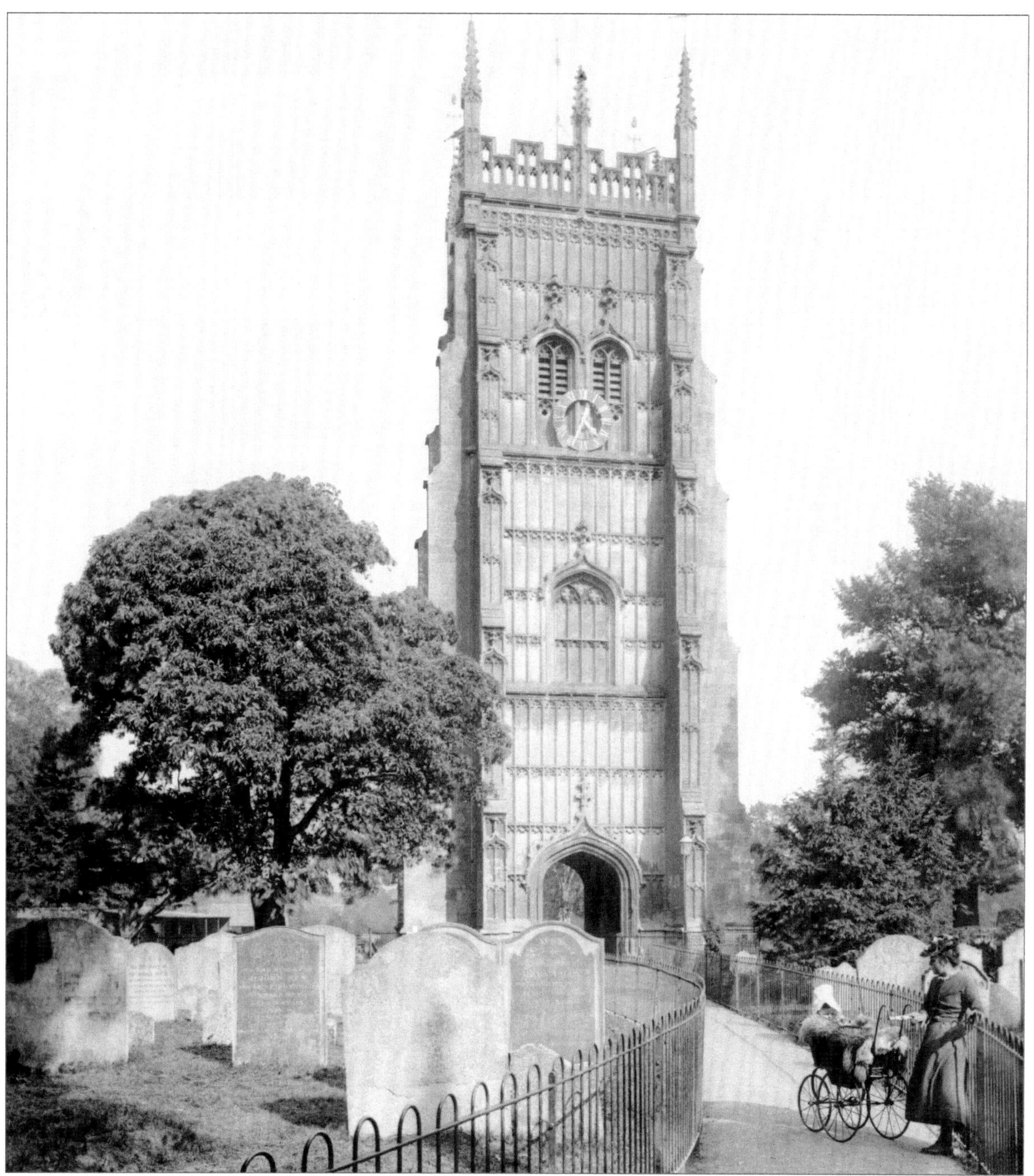

THE BELL TOWER *1892* 31094

This masterpiece of Perpendicular architecture was begun by Abbot Clement Lichfield in 1533 and completed in 1538, only months before the Dissolution. Its purpose was not only to house the abbey bells, but also to form a gatehouse to the cemetery. The tower was bought by the town in the 1540s, reputedly for £100.

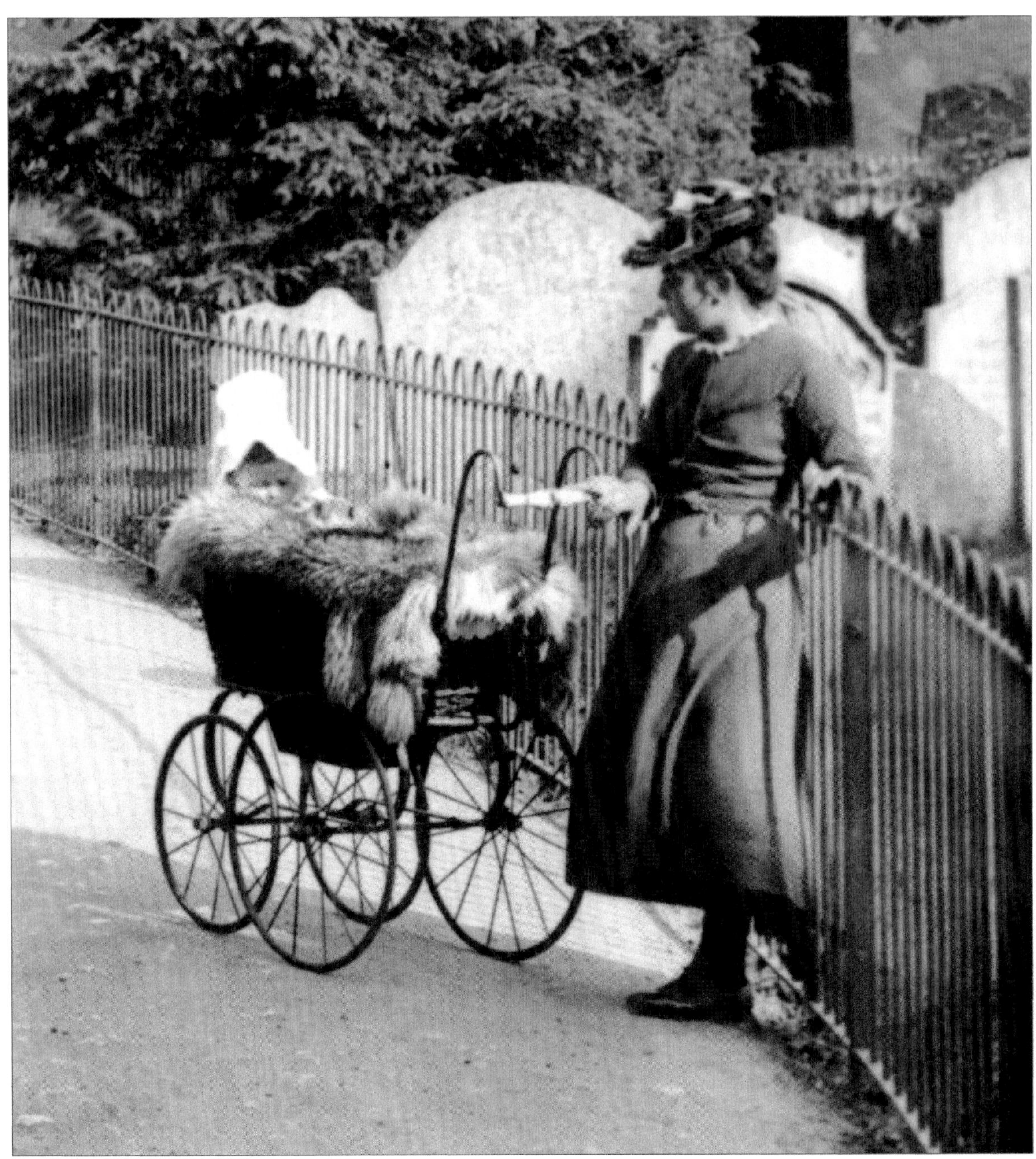

WOMAN AND CHILD, *Near the Bell Tower 1892* 31094x

It is impossible to say whether the woman in this charming detail from 31094 (on the previous page) is the mother of the child in the pram or its nanny, but perhaps the latter is more likely - the fur cover draped over the child suggests a degree of affluence. The railings against which the woman is leaning have long since been removed. Sad to say, so have most of the headstones.

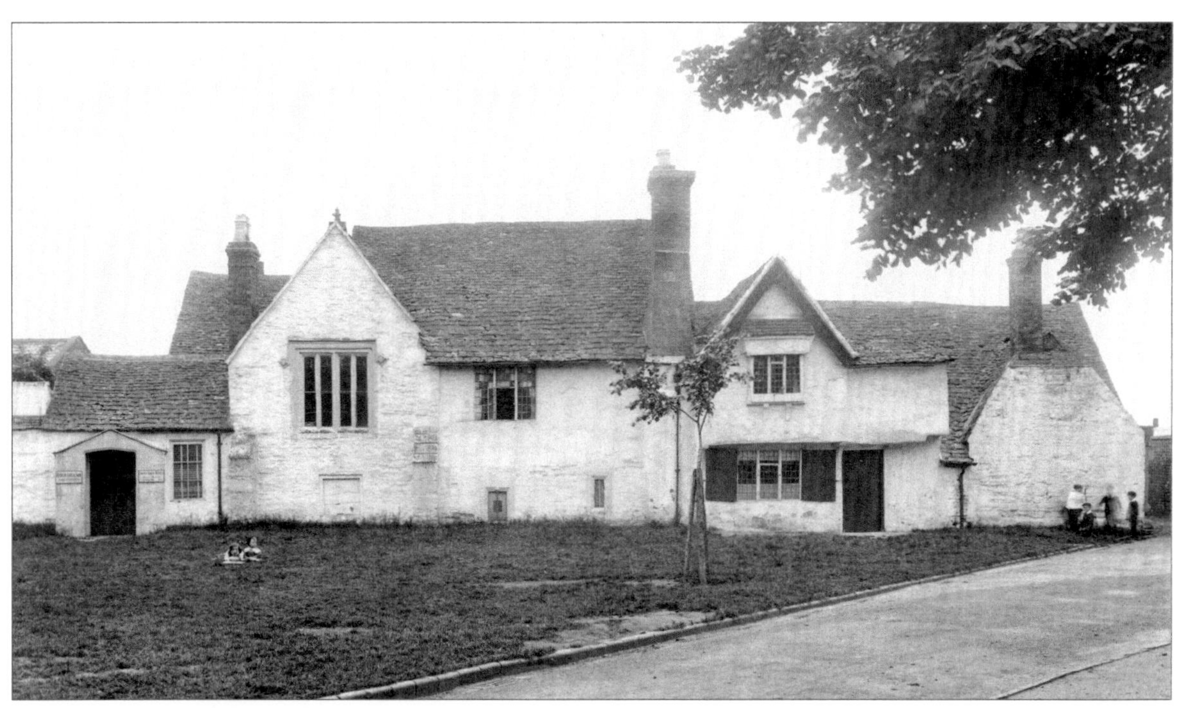

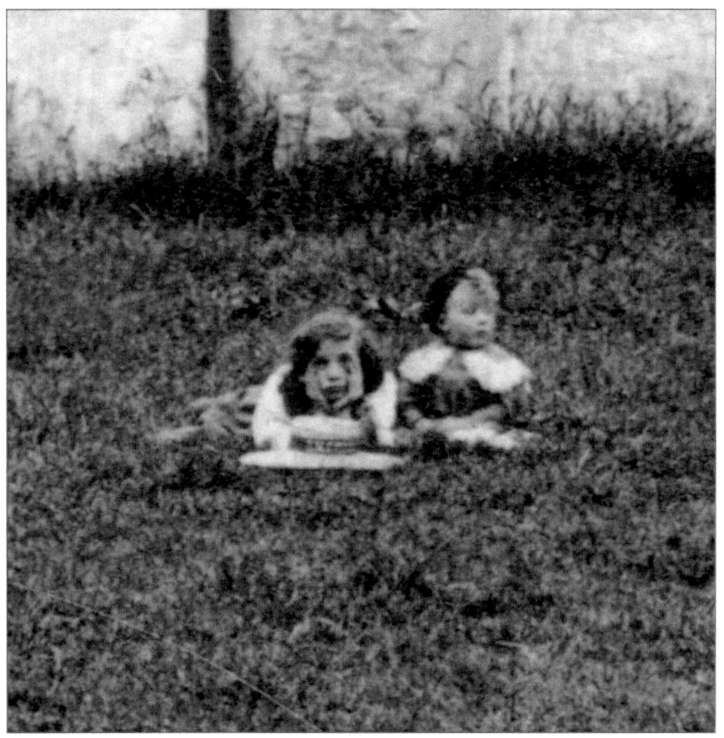

▲ **THE OLD ALMONRY** *1910* 62346

This building stands just outside Abbey Gate, and is probably another survivor of the monastic foundation, for it is believed to have been the home of the almoner, the official responsible for the distribution of alms to the poor. It was incumbent upon larger Benedictine foundations to help the poor and hungry.

◀ *detail from* 62346

THE ALMONRY
1931 84575a

With its timbers revealed, the Almonry in this 1930s photograph is quite changed from its appearance in 1910 (see 62346, previous page). It still looks like this today, but the tea rooms which it housed in 1931 have long gone, and it is now the Almonry Heritage Centre, comprising a tourist information centre and a fascinating museum. The 700-year-old building is itself the museum's finest exhibit.

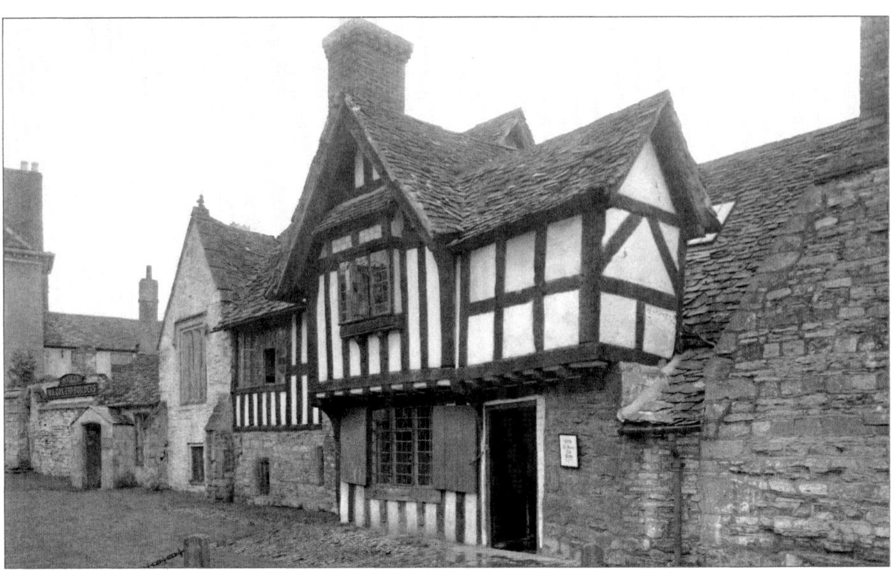

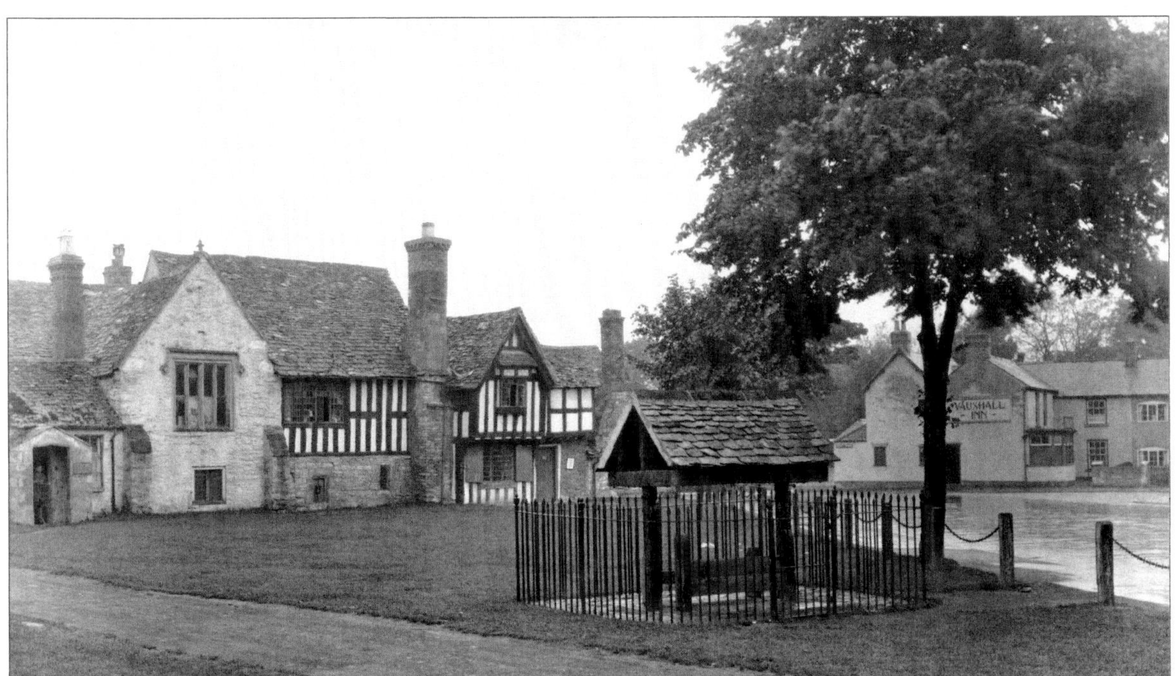

THE OLD STOCKS AND THE ALMONRY *1931* 84576

When the abbey was suppressed the almonry was leased to the last abbot. After his death it continued in use as a private house until it was sold to Evesham Corporation in 1929 by the Rudge family. The intention was always to use it as a museum, but it was not until 1957 that the Almonry Museum opened. It became the Almonry Heritage Centre in 1995, and it is run by the town council in conjunction with the Vale of Evesham Historical Society. The stocks were placed here in the 1920s after being removed from the gaol which was formerly attached to the Town Hall.

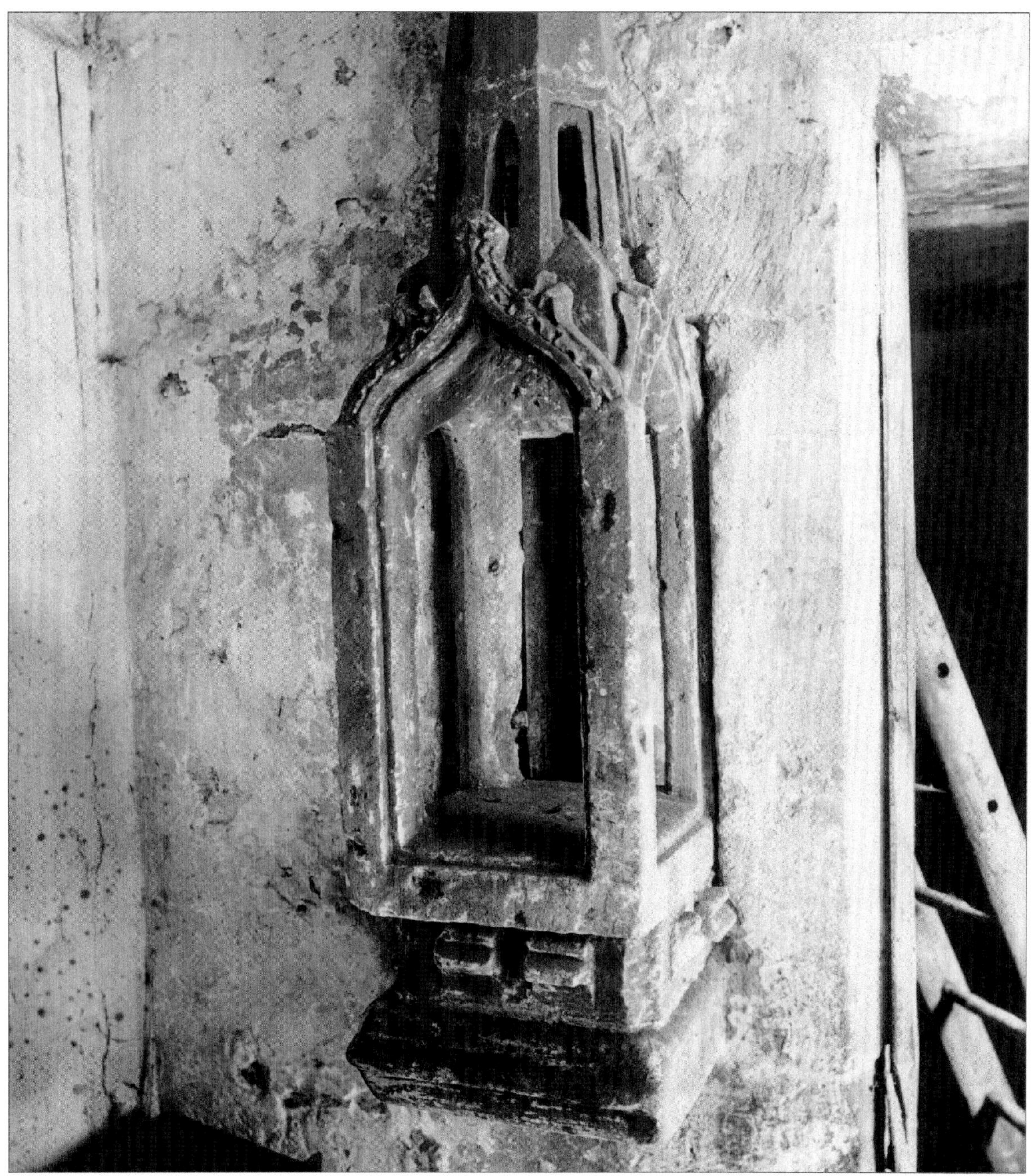

THE ALMONRY, *The Old Lantern 1892* 31100

A colour photograph of this 15th-century stone lantern or lamp-niche is used by the Almonry Heritage Centre in its promotional leaflet. The lantern is just one of thousands of items of interest in the museum's collection, which contains everything from agricultural tools to Saxon burial goods to the town charter granted to Evesham in 1604.

MARKET PLACE, HIGH STREET AND VINE STREET

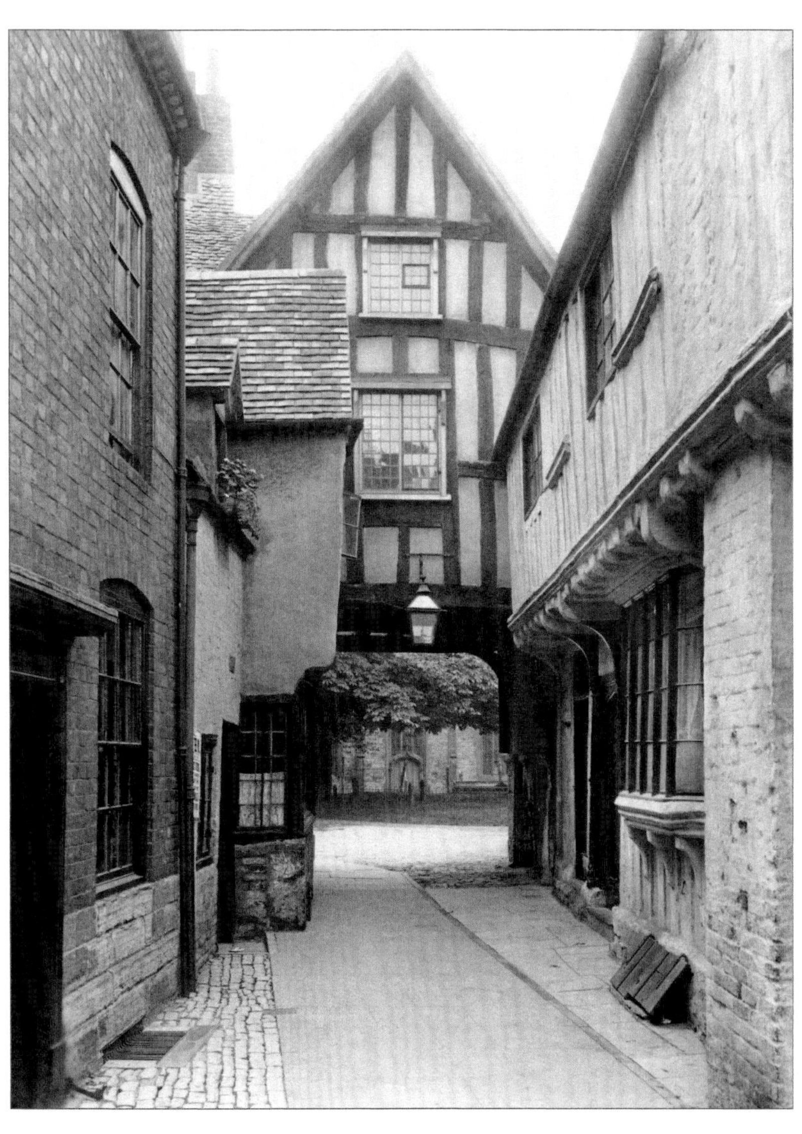

ABBOT REGINALD'S GATEWAY *1892* 31104

This passageway (which is seen from the other side in 36962 on page 15) provided the quickest approach to the abbey from Market Place. The building on the right is the 15th-century Walker Hall, which was purchased and reconstructed as a parish hall by means of funds raised by James Manders Walker, vicar of Evesham 1900-1919. When he died in 1929 he left £200 to the trustees for its upkeep on condition that it should be known as the Walker Hall. It was recently restored again, with the assistance of English Heritage, and won an award for distinction from Wychavon District Council in 2001.

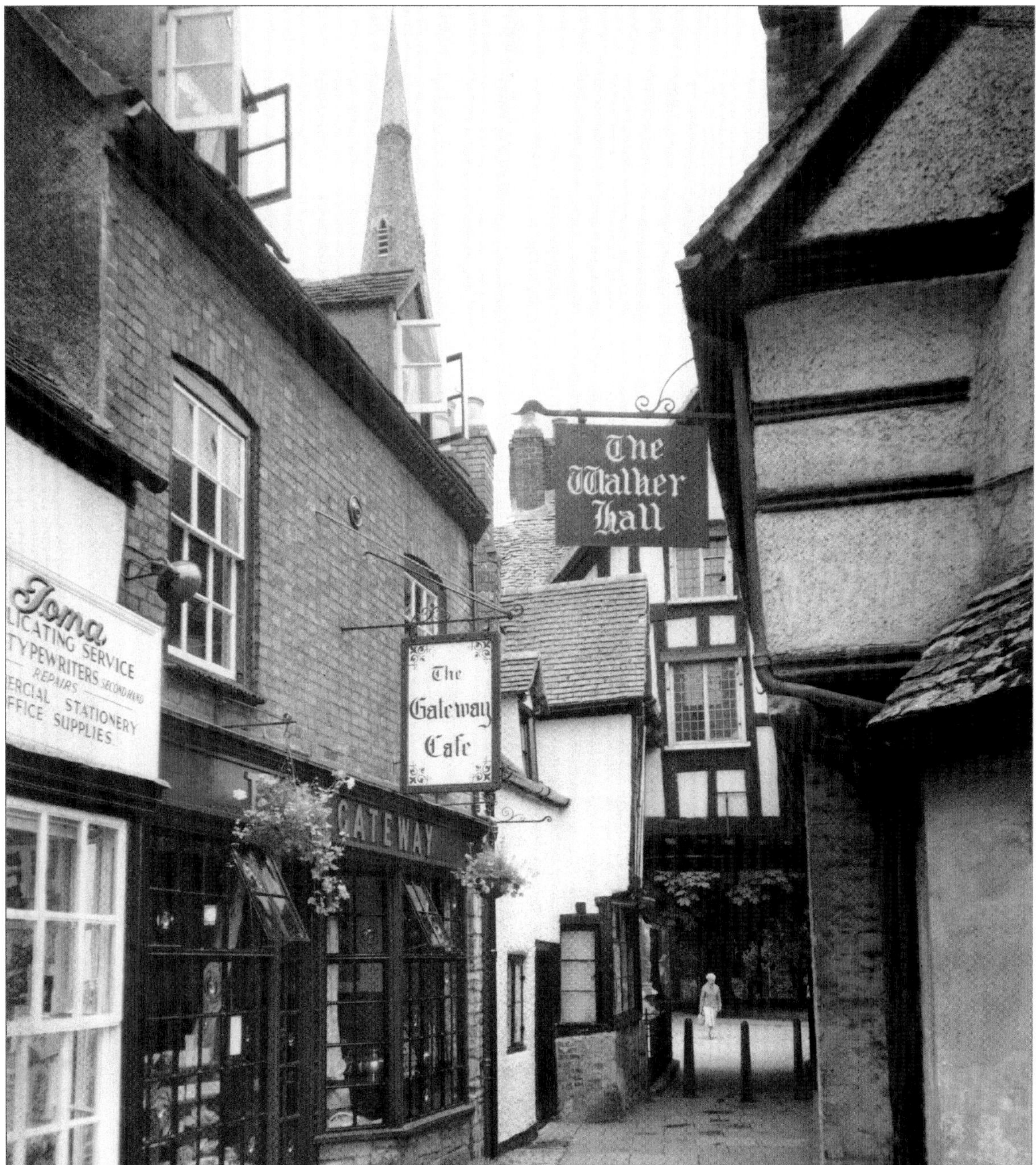

ABBOT REGINALD'S GATEWAY *c1960* E44101

Close comparison with 31104 (opposite) shows that the intervening 68 years had brought only small changes, such as the ground-floor windows for the Gateway Café (which is still trading today). The bollards suggest that people had been in the habit of driving through the archway, in the days when Market Place remained open to traffic.

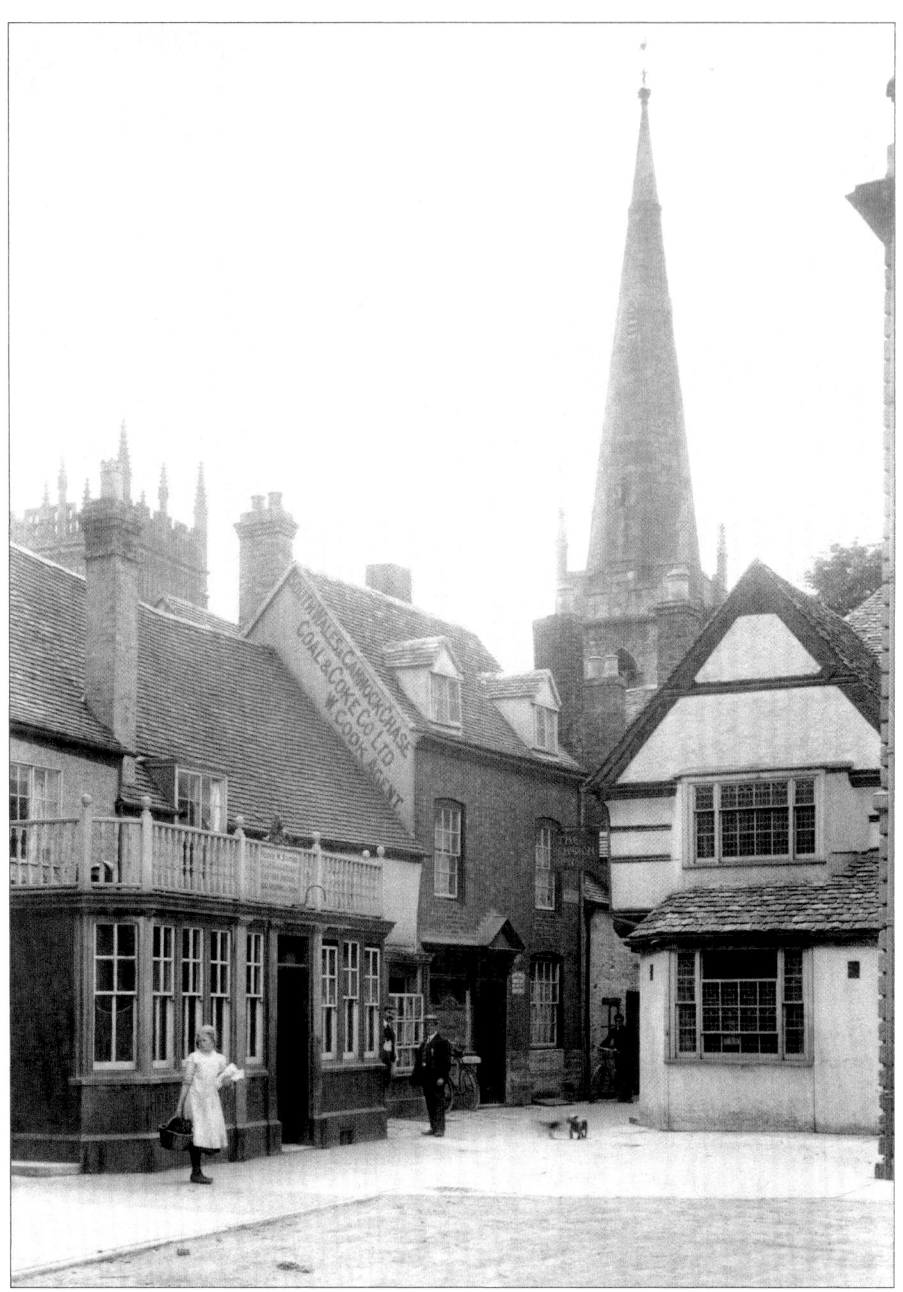

MARKET PLACE *1910* 62349

The passageway leaving the south-east corner of Market Place leads to Abbot Reginald's Gateway, and the building on the right was later to become the Walker Hall. How sad it is that the building on the left has lost its attractive balcony and windows. It was a pub at the time of this photograph, known as the Red Lion and run by Frederick W Stafford. It is now Evesham Appliance Centre, selling white goods. The building in the centre was occupied by a coal and coke agent, but later became the Gateway Café.

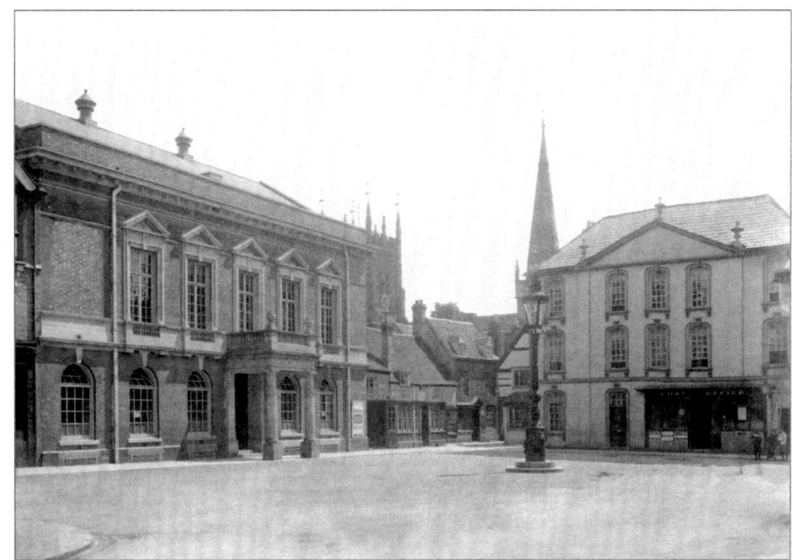

MARKET PLACE *1910* 62344

The neo-Georgian Public Hall on the left was built 1908-09; it also had to accommodate the library, which vacated cramped premises elsewhere. In 1975 part of the library's stock moved to the Walker Hall, and the rest went to the Town Hall in 1989 when Abbey Gate Shopping Centre (now Riverside) was built behind the Public Hall - the façade of which was retained to form one of the entrances. The library finally got its own purpose-built premises on Oat Street in 1990. The lovely building on the right housed the post office until 1960 when it moved to High Street, and this building suffered changes which make it barely recognisable today.

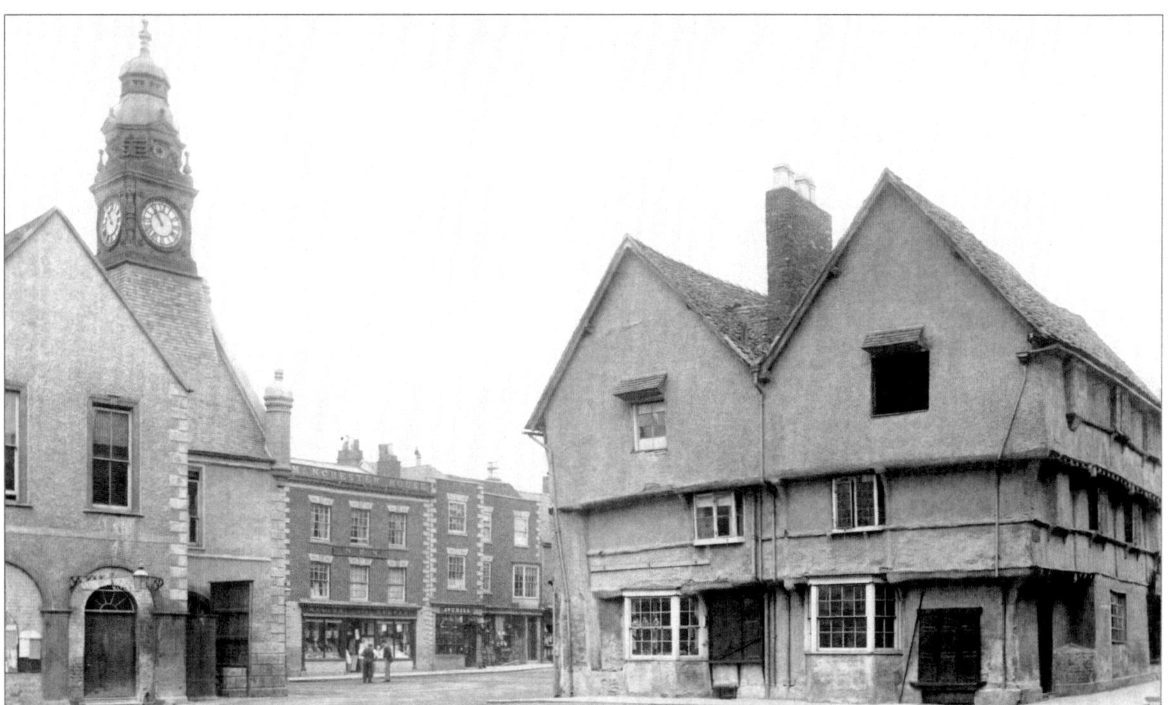

MARKET PLACE *1892* 31102

The Town Hall, on the extreme left, was built in 1586 with stone from the abbey, and remodelled 1884-85. It has since been extended, partially blocking the view to High Street, where the fine building on the left was Manchester House, demolished in 1931 for road widening. A replacement, with a curved frontage, was erected (see E44072, page 46). Booth Hall, on the right, has now been restored to timber-framed glory.

▼ BOOTH HALL *1931* 84575

This is usually known as the Round House, for reasons which are unclear, but one thing is for sure: this is a very fortunate building. In the 1960s, when Britain was engaged in wholesale demolition of its architectural heritage, the 15th-century Booth Hall was sensitively restored instead. The National Provincial Bank had bought it in 1919, and since 1970 it has been occupied by NatWest Bank (the result of a merger between National Provincial Bank and Westminster Bank). Journal Buildings, on the left, was owned in 1931 by W and H Smith, publishers of the Evesham Journal. It was later purchased, oddly enough, by W H Smith & Son, which occupies it still.

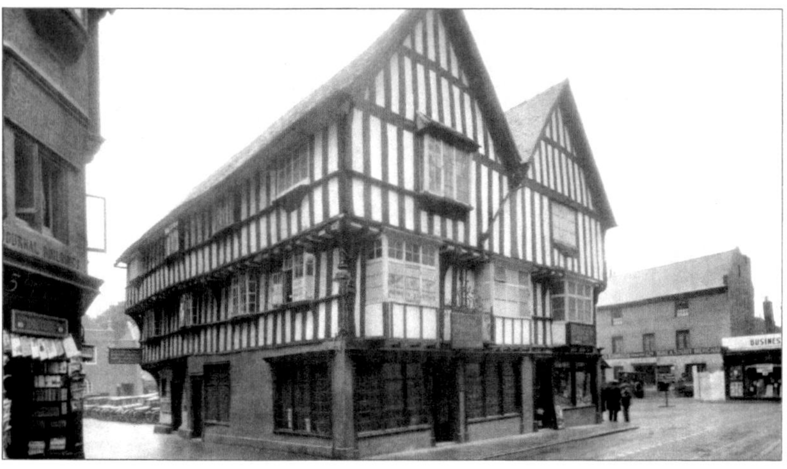

▼ BOOTH HALL *c1960* E44118

Booth Hall dominates Market Place, which by 1960 had suffered the fate of so many former market places (and village greens) all over the country: it had been turned into a car park. However, Evesham was ultimately luckier than most of its counterparts. In 1989, when Abbey Gate Shopping Centre opened, Market Place was restored and pedestrianised.

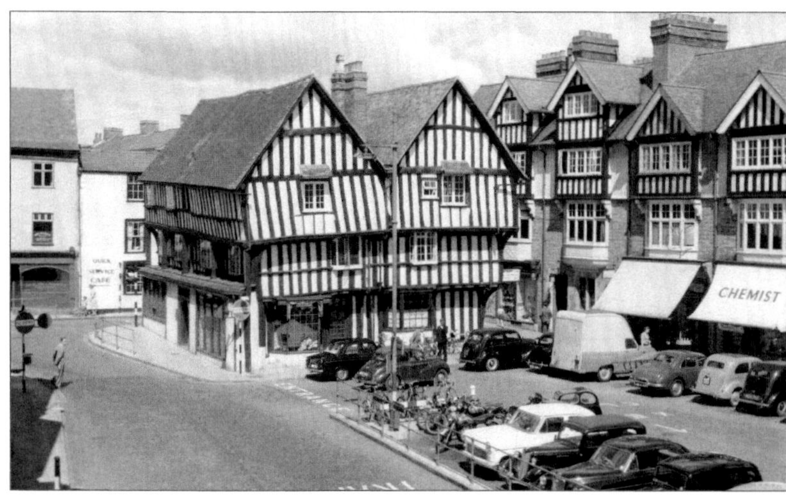

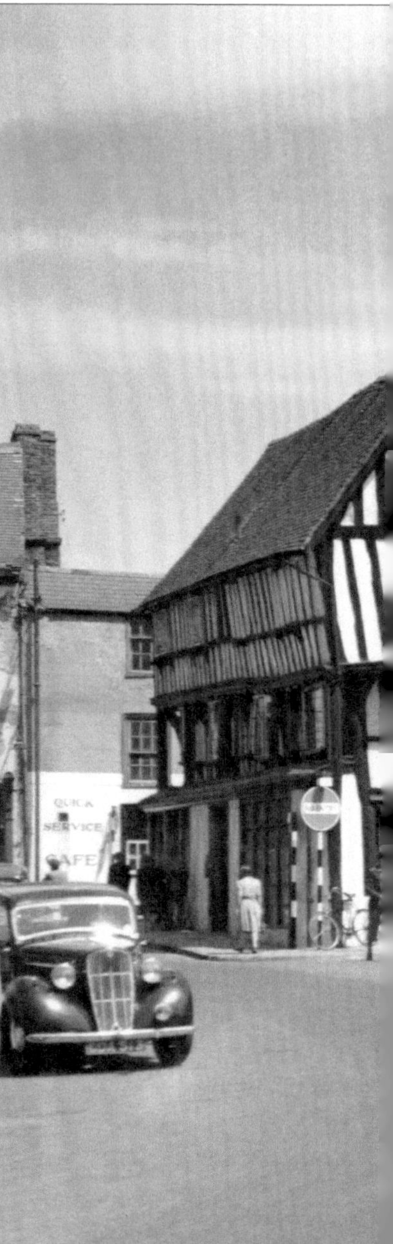

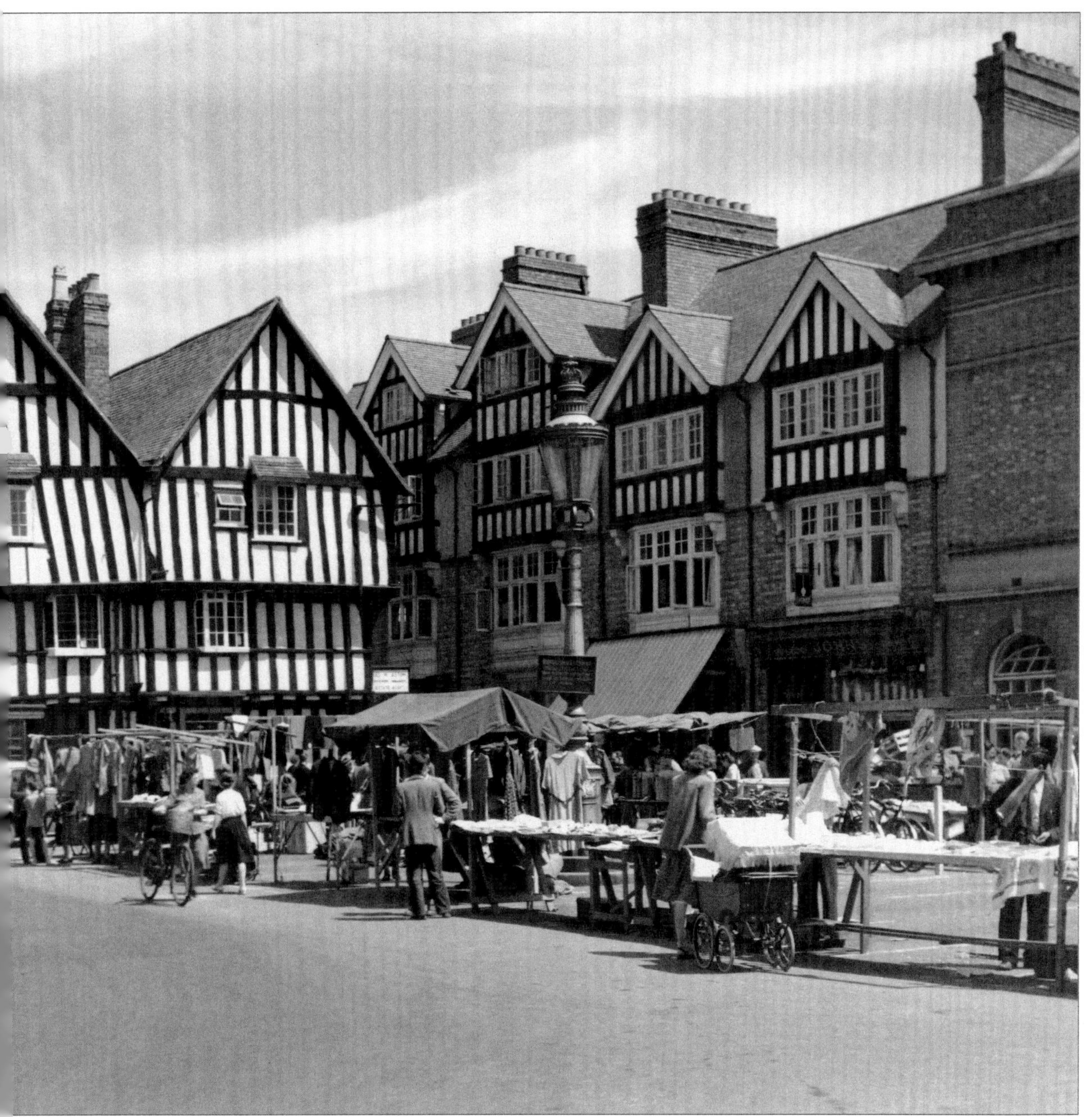

▲ **MARKET PLACE AND BOOTH HALL** *c1955* E44069

Market Place was still only lightly used by traffic at this time, and the market was still a popular event. Produce had been sold in the streets and in Market Place for centuries, but in the 1880s the vale's smallholders won the right to have thrice-weekly auctions here, in order to secure faster sales and better prices for their produce.

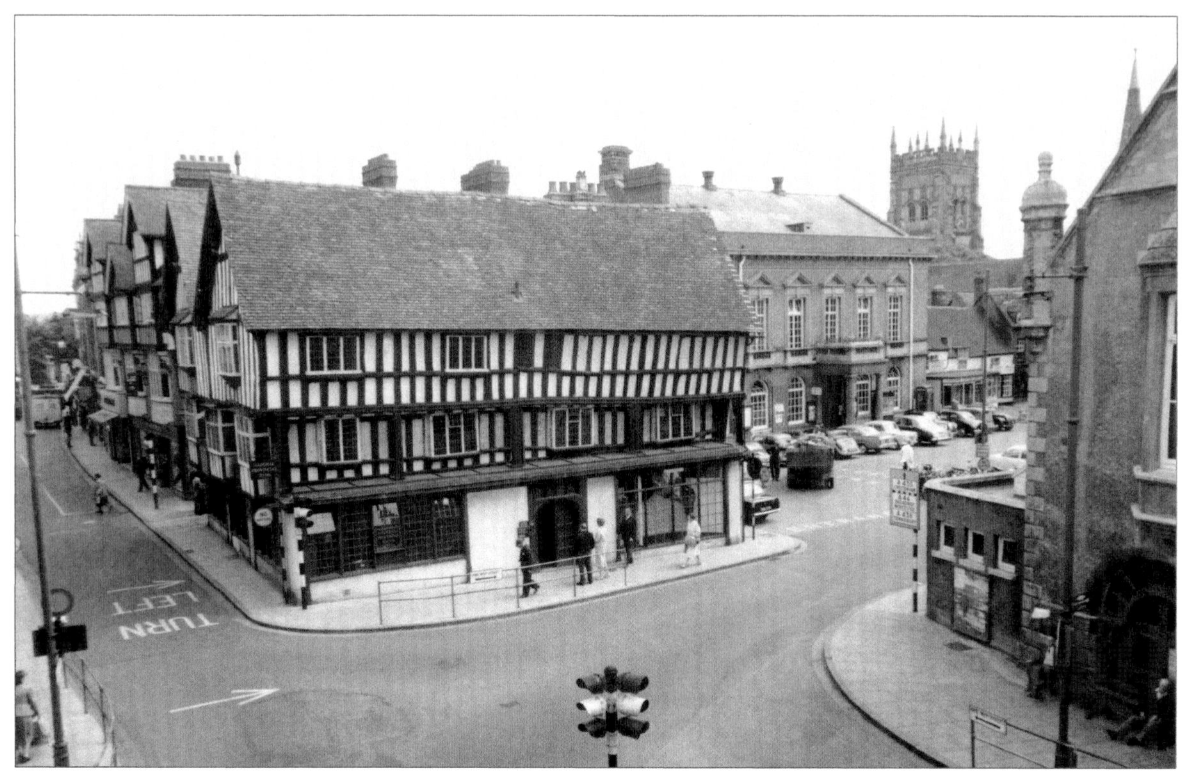

BOOTH HALL AND MARKET PLACE *c1965* E44104

The traffic sign to the left of the Town Hall indicates that
Market Place was still a through route in 1965. Nowadays traffic
passes to the right of the Town Hall instead, along Vine Street,
which was widened for the purpose. Booth Hall was restored
1963-65. At the time of this photograph, much more remained to
be done, including the addition of two windows to the
upper storey.

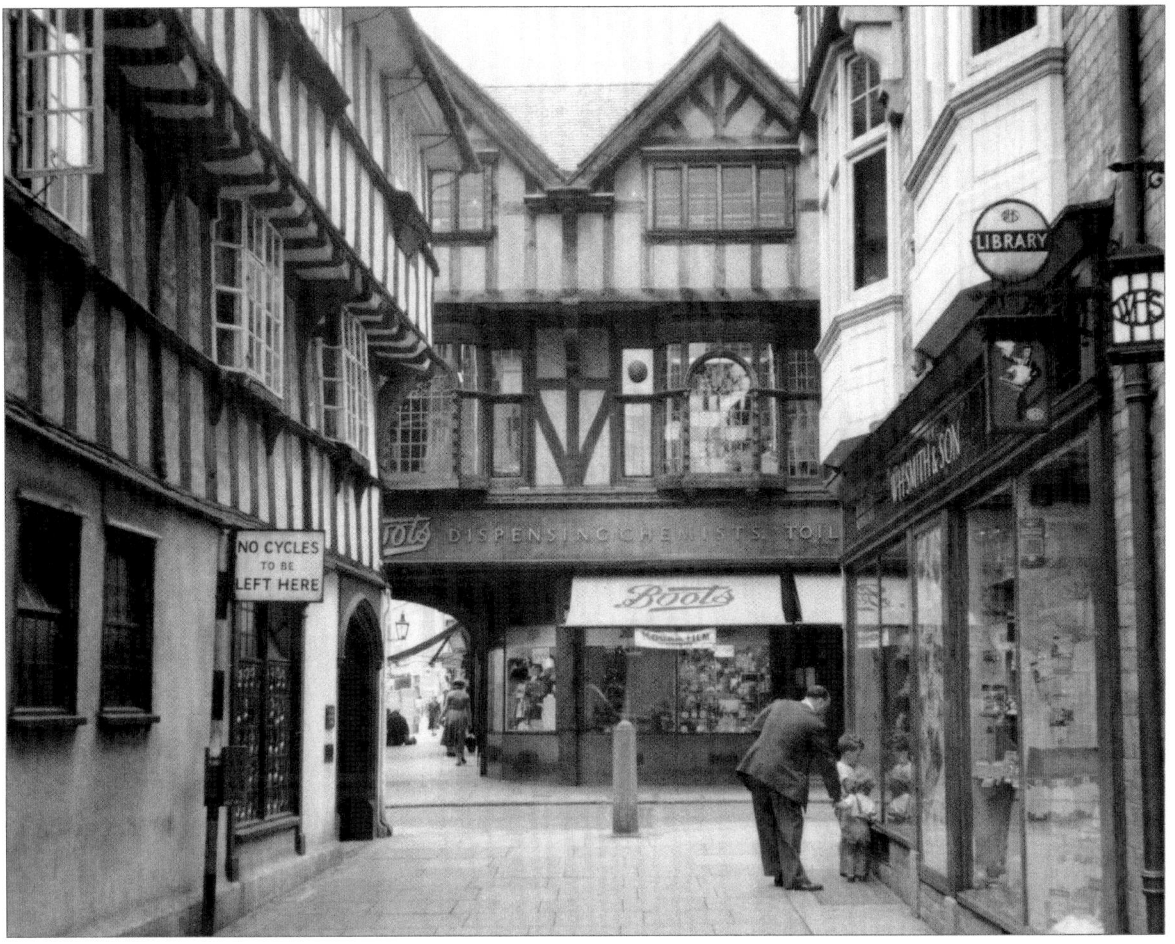

BOOTH HALL *c1965* E44100

Booth Hall is on the left here, facing W H Smith across
Melsungen Allee (named after Evesham's German twin). Notice
Smith's old-style sign, together with a library sign. What were
known as circulating libraries were started in 1858 by
W H Smith II to help satisfy a growing demand for fiction among
an increasingly literate public. Boots the Chemists (centre) also
operated libraries. Improved provision of local authority library
services put an end to circulating libraries in the early 1960s.
W H Smith still occupies this same site, but Boots has moved
further down Bridge Street.

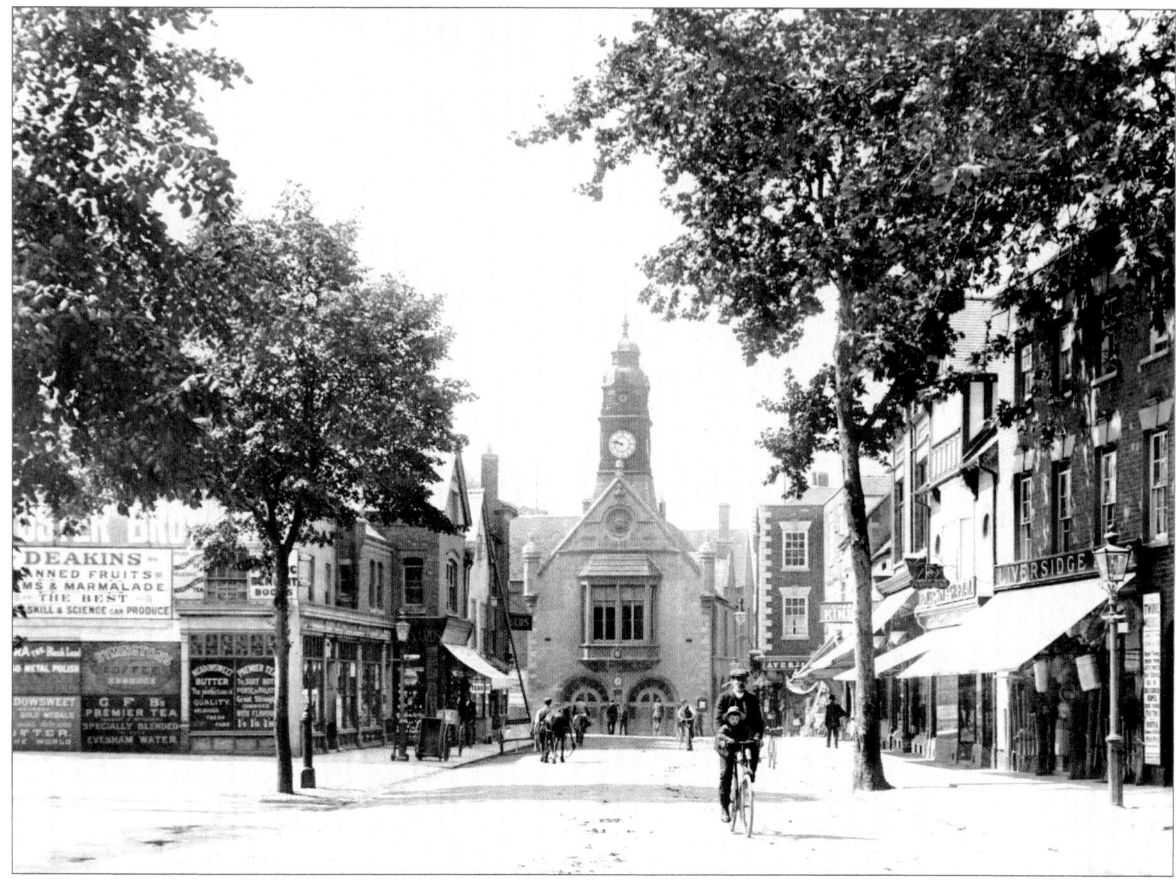

HIGH STREET

1910 62339

Though the Town Hall is instantly recognisable, the overall
scene has greatly changed. Traffic dominates now, along with a
plethora of traffic-related clutter. Manchester House, to the right
of the Town Hall, was demolished in 1931 for road widening. The
buildings on the left, with their fascinating advertisements (for
canned fruits, marmalade, metal polish, butter, coffee and tea)
have been replaced by an ugly flat-roofed structure.

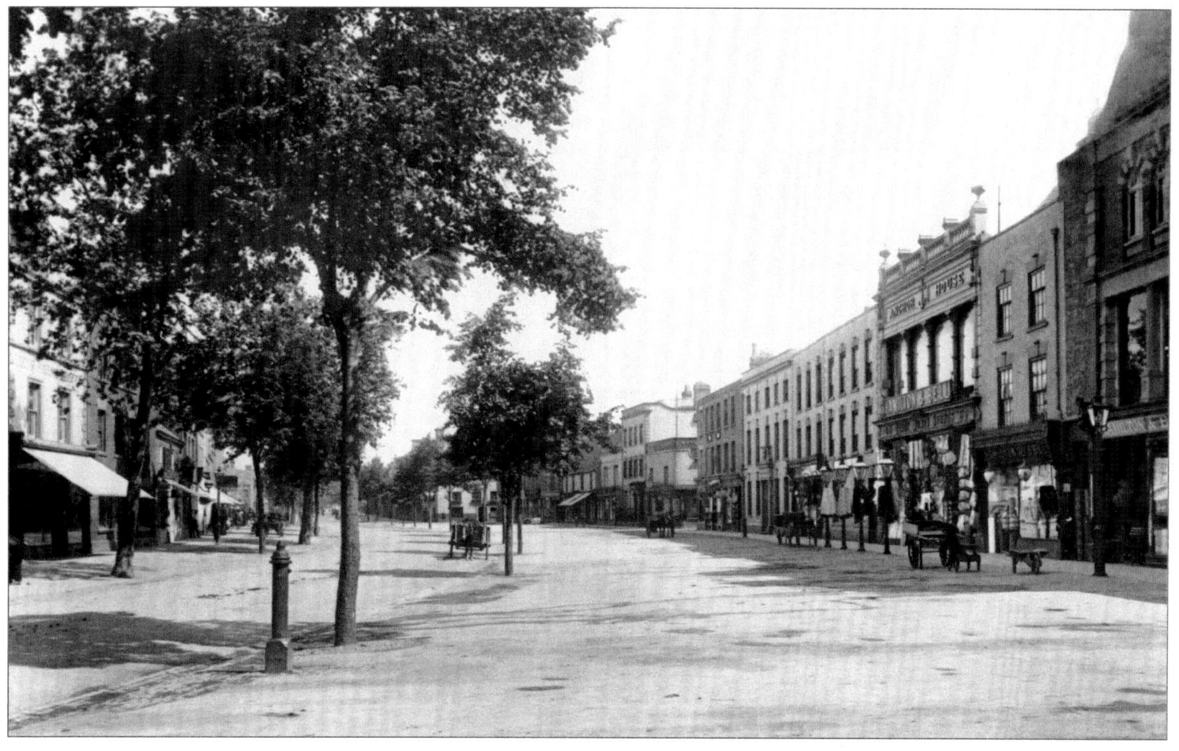

HIGH STREET
1910 62338

Evesham's main street is long and unusually broad, as this photograph suggests. It was the venue for a weekly cattle market until 1880, when a purpose-built cattle market was provided in a more convenient location. The buildings along the east side of High Street reflect the predominantly Georgian nature of the town, which still persists today.

HIGH STREET
c1960 E44119

Though the buildings are not greatly changed from 1910 (62338, page 33), the motor car has now taken over. Pedestrians are banished to the margins of the wide highway, which has become not only a busy road but a car park too. It also has to accommodate a bus station, which occupies the area towards the back of this picture, on the right.

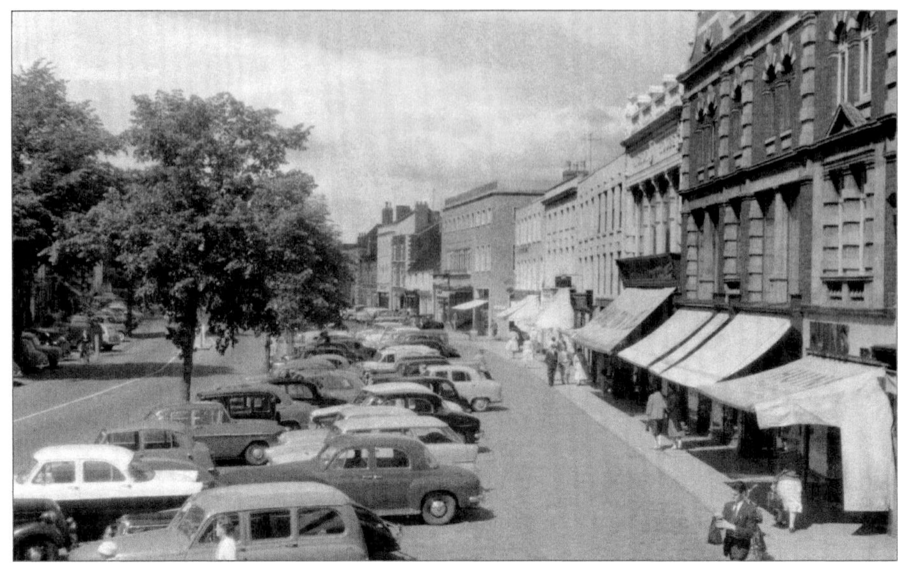

VINE STREET
1922 72430

Vine Street, effectively the southern continuation of High Street, was originally Swine Street, because pigs were sold there in the Middle Ages. One would have to stand on a traffic island today to photograph this view towards the town centre. The building on the left is Ye Olde Red Horse, before the plaster was removed in 1932 to expose its 16th-century timbers.

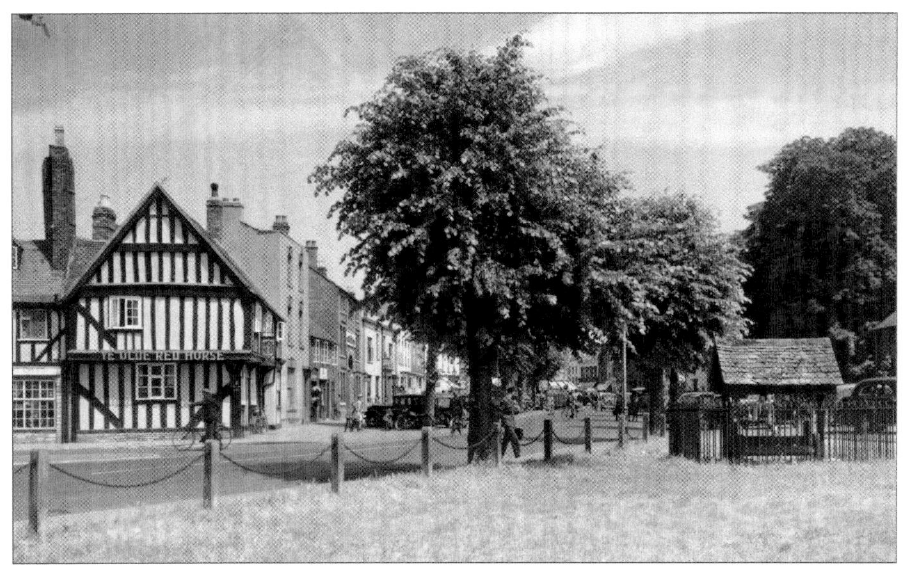

VINE STREET AND THE STOCKS
c1955 E44068

Ye Olde Red Horse looks better than it did in 1922 (72430, page 34). It can be a mistake to reveal hidden timbers, which were not always meant to be seen. These, however, are decorative as well as structural, and were clearly meant to be exposed. Such close-studding was the preserve of the wealthy, who liked the world to see that they could afford to use timber lavishly.

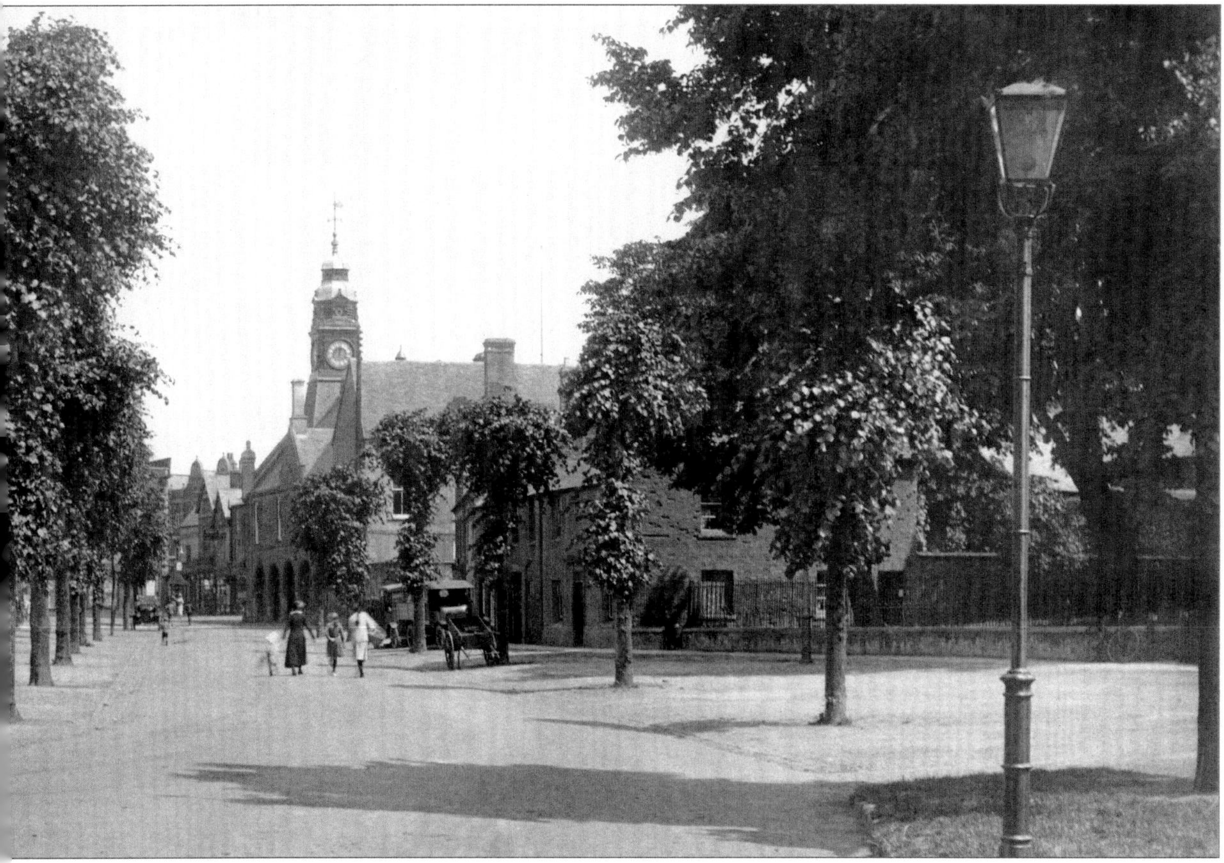

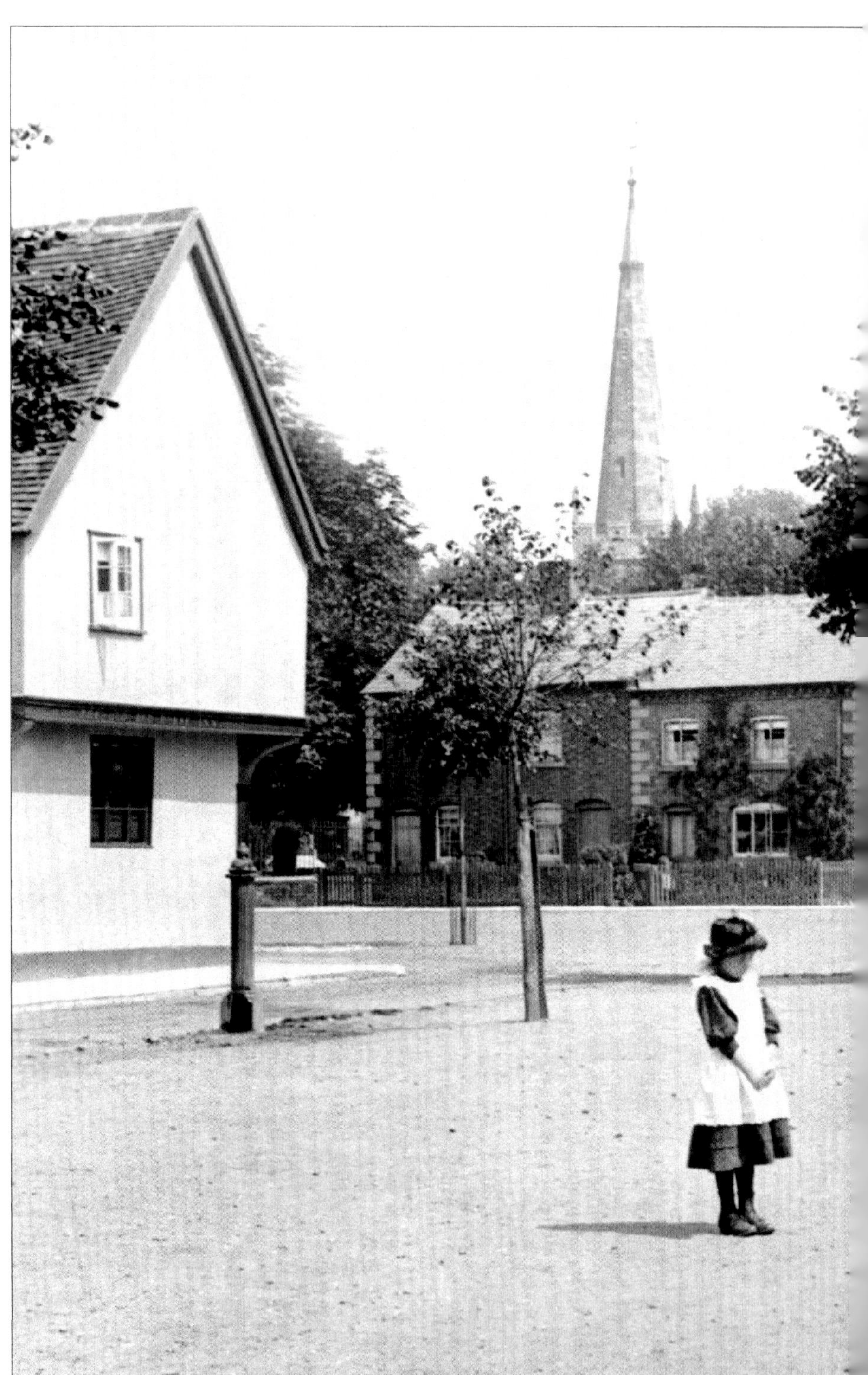

MERSTOW GREEN
1892 31089

Merstow Green, just off Vine Street, really was a green, complete with trees, even into the 1960s. Nikolaus Pevsner, in 'The Buildings of England: Worcestershire' (1968), wrote 'This is an asset Evesham must retain and cultivate. Car parking has already reduced its amenity considerably.' But Evesham took no notice of Pevsner, and Merstow Green is now a particularly ugly road junction.

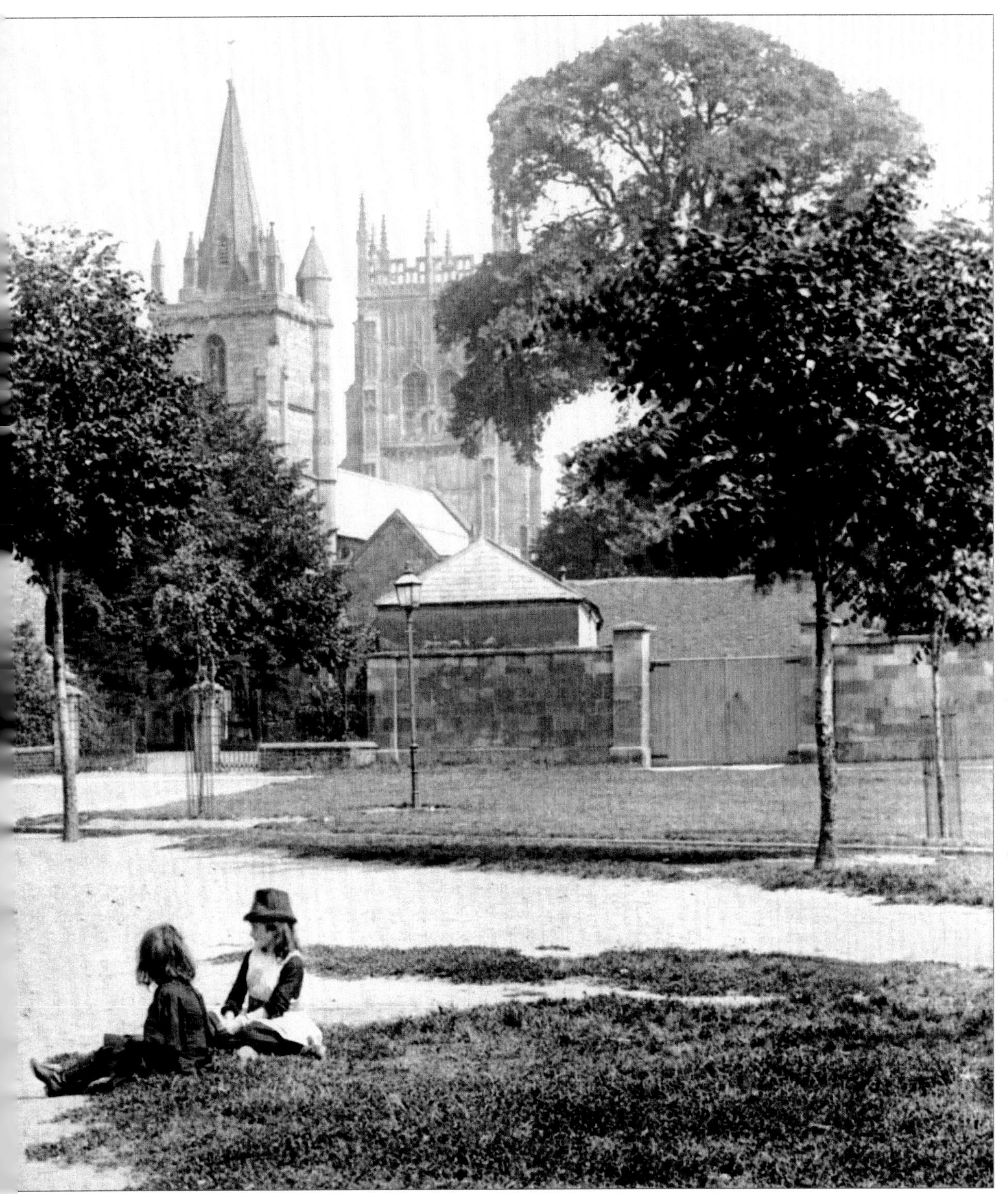

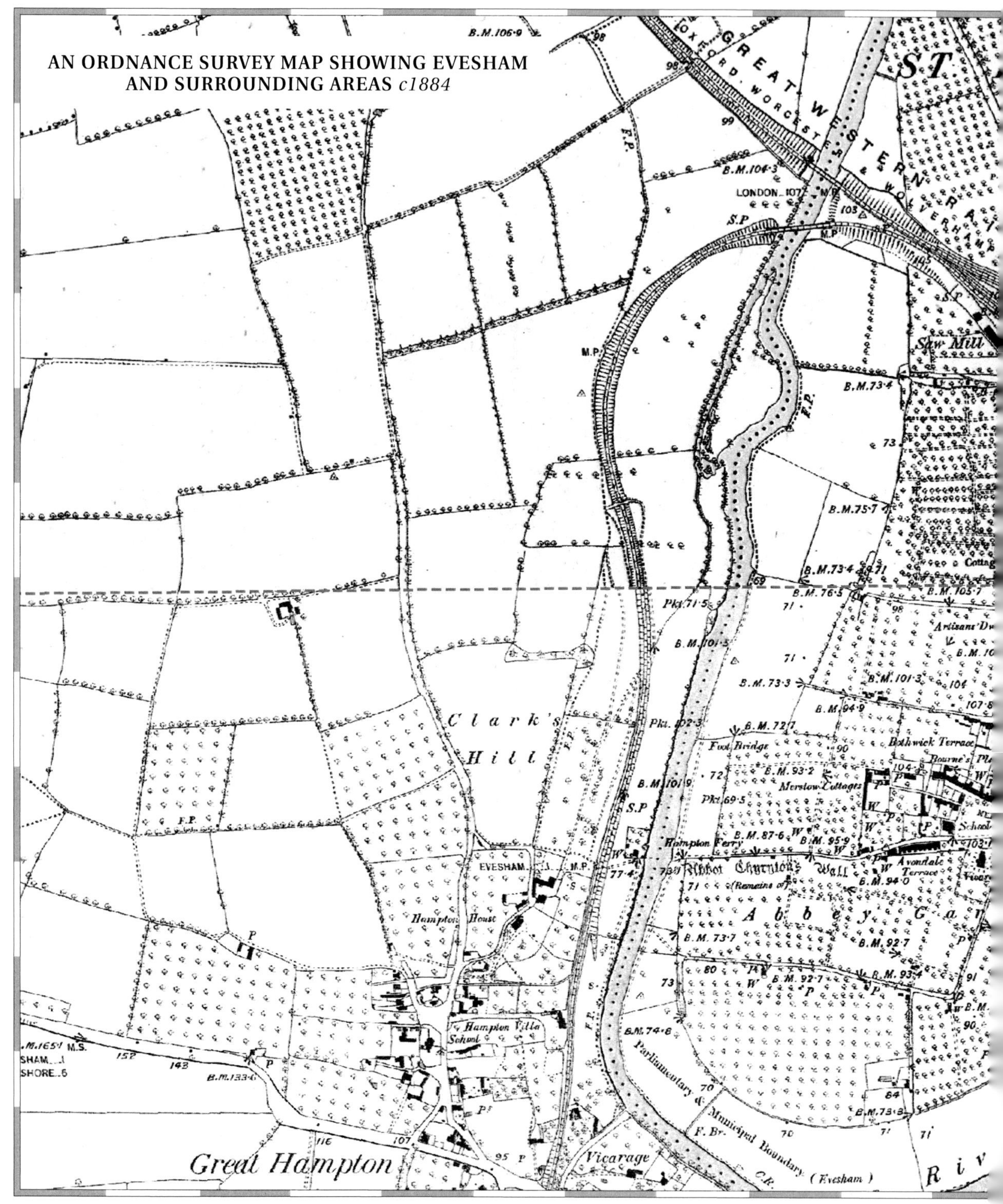
AN ORDNANCE SURVEY MAP SHOWING EVESHAM
AND SURROUNDING AREAS c1884

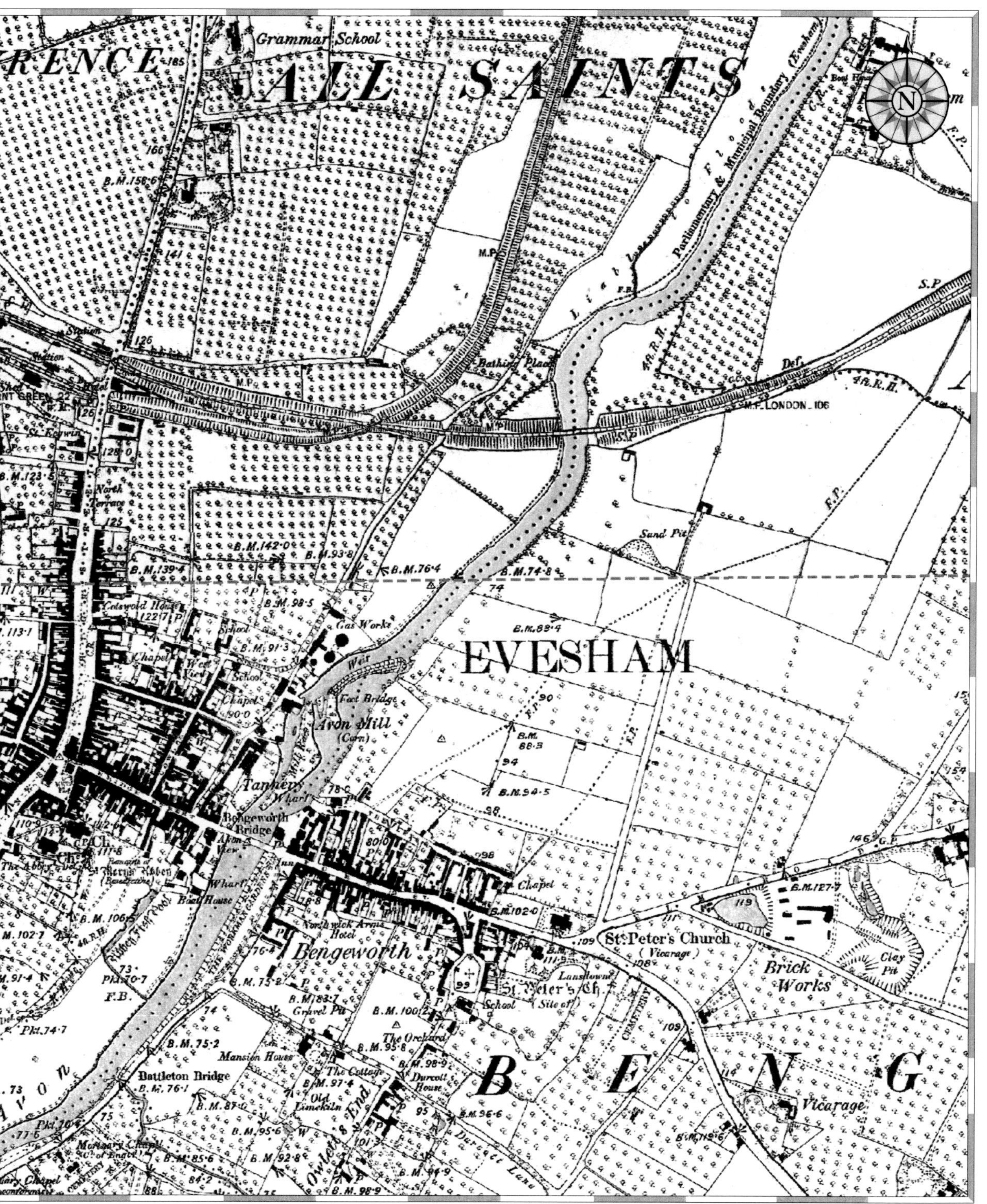

Grammar School
RENCE
ALL SAINTS
185
166
B.M.158·6
141
M.P
Lidd
Parliamentary & Municipal Boundary (Evesham)
Boat Hou
N
S.P
Station
126
Bathing Place
Def
M.F. LONDON_106
S.E. Road
NT GREEN 22
126
St. Edwin
126·0
North
Terrace
125
Sand Pit
S.P
B.M.123
B.M.142·0
B.M.93·8
B.M.76·4
B.M.74·8
74
B.M.139·4
EVESHAM
113·1
Cotswold House
122·7 P
B.M.98·5
B.M.83·4
School
Gas Works
Chapel
B.M.91·3
Weir
90
School
B.M.
88·3
Chapel
90·0
Foot Bridge
94
Avon Mill
(Corn)
B.M.94·5
98
Tannery
Wharf
78·0
Bengeworth
Bridge
80·0
98
110·9
P Ch
Chapel
B.M.102·0
St. Peter's Church
(Vicarage)
The Abbey
Remains of
Abbey
Benedictine
Wharf
119
B.M.127·7
Boat House
B.M.106·2
St. Peter's Ch.
Clay
Pit
M.102·7
46 R.H.
Landsdown
Brick
Works
73
Pkt 70·7
F.B.
76·1
Bengeworth
99
St. Peter's Ch.
School
Site of
109
M.91·4
B.M.75·2
B.M.183·7
Gravel Pit
B.M.100·2
114
Pkt.74·7
74
Vicarage
B.M.75·2
Mansion House
The Orchard
B.M.95·8
B.M.98·9
B.M.112·6
73
Battleton Bridge
B.M.76·1
The Cottage
B.M.97·4
Durcott
House
Owler's End
BENG
Pkt.70·7
71·6
Old
Limekiln
95
B.M.96·6
Marian's Chapel
R. of Engl.
75
B.M.95·6
B.M.92·8
101·3
Durcott Land
nconformist
88
84·2
76
B.M.98·9
B.M.84·9

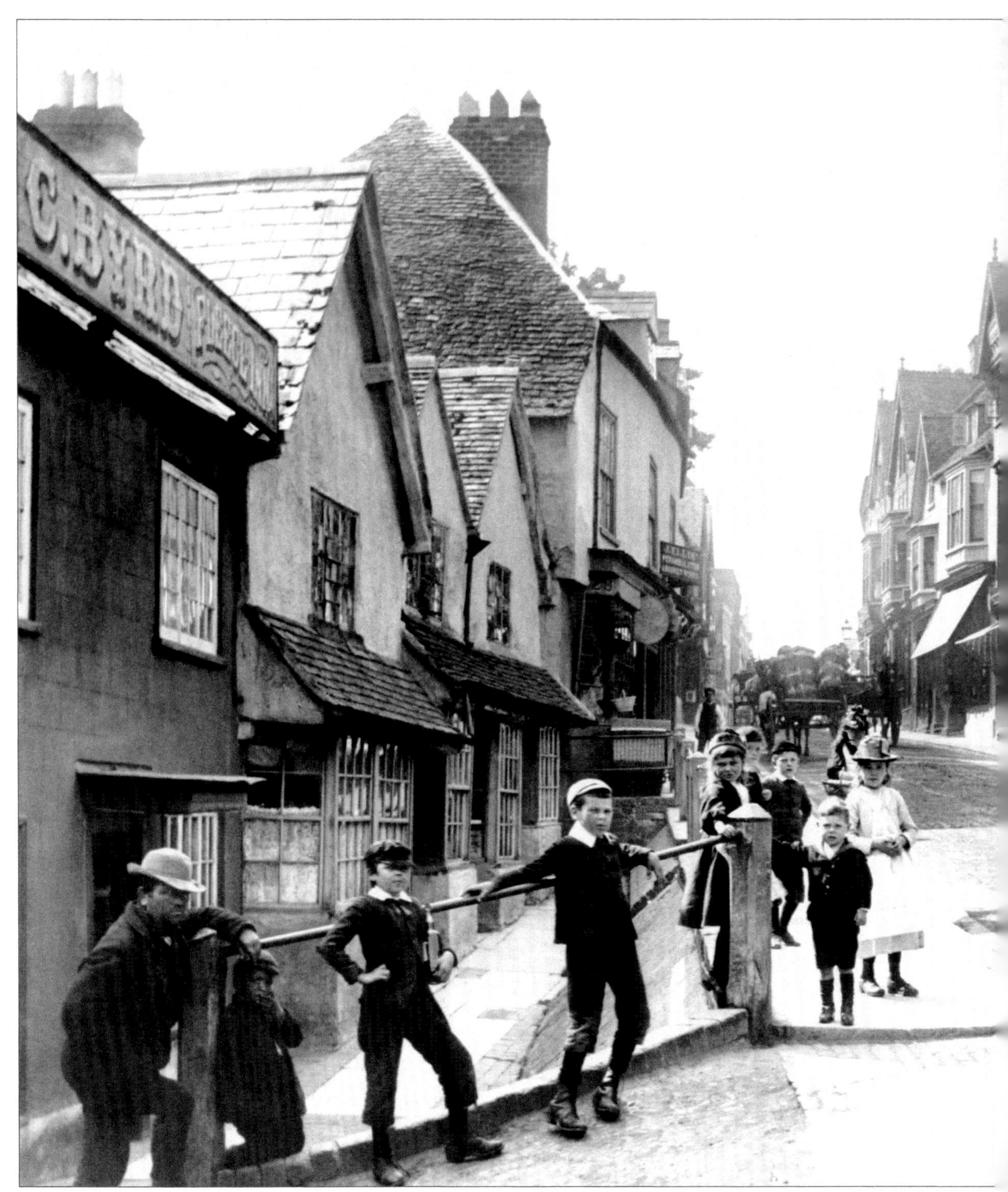
C. BYRD

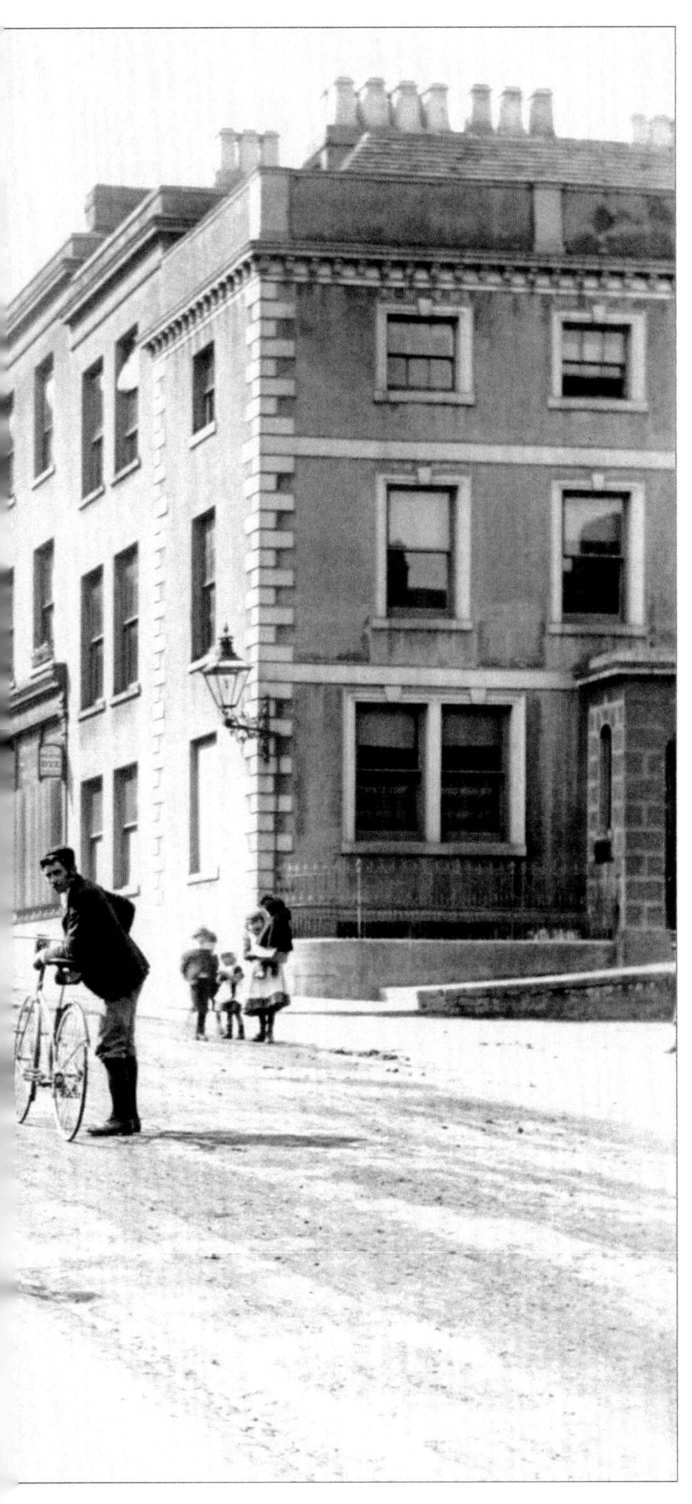

BRIDGE STREET, ABBEY PARK AND THE RIVER AVON

BRIDGE STREET *1892* 31106

Bridge Street runs down to Workman Bridge (Evesham Bridge until 1855) which spans the Avon to link Evesham with Bengeworth, on the other side of the river. This view is taken from the bridge, looking uphill towards the town centre, and it is apparent from the demeanour of both children and adults that a photographer was a comparatively rare sight at this time.

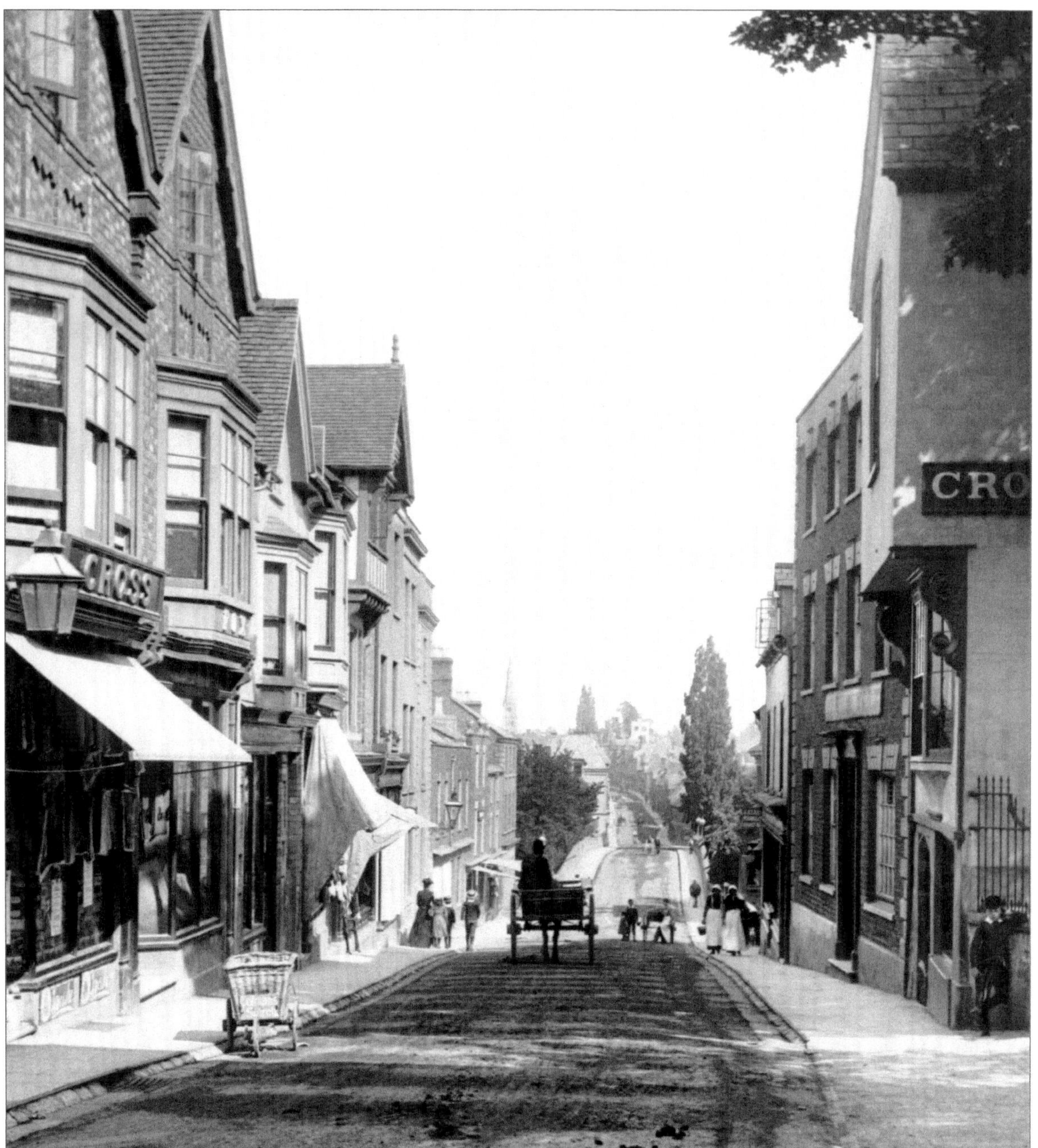

BRIDGE STREET *1892* 31105

The former Crown Hotel is just visible on the right in this view, which was taken looking downhill towards the bridge. The wicker handcart by the kerb and the horse-drawn cart further down the street speak of more peaceful days when delivery and distribution were on a smaller scale. Bridge Street, however, is again pleasantly free of traffic since its pedestrianisation in 1997.

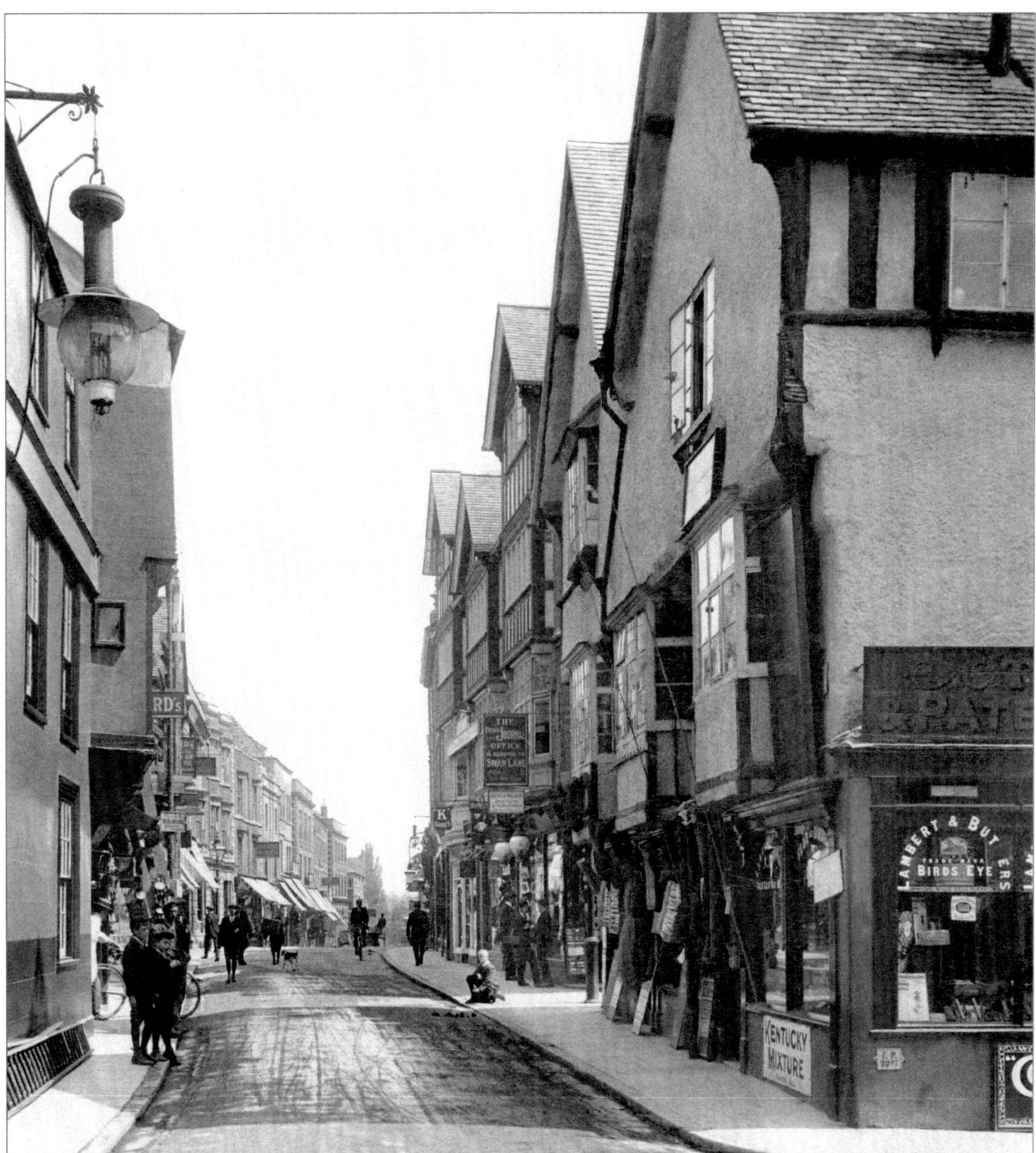

BRIDGE STREET *1910* 62342

It is impossible to identify this scene with any confidence today. Maybe these buildings were demolished to make way for Abbey Gate (now Riverside), a shopping development which opened in 1989. In some respects, it is a relatively innocuous specimen of its kind, making little impression on Bridge Street or Market Place. It is very sad that the same cannot be said of its impact on Abbey Park, which is considerable.

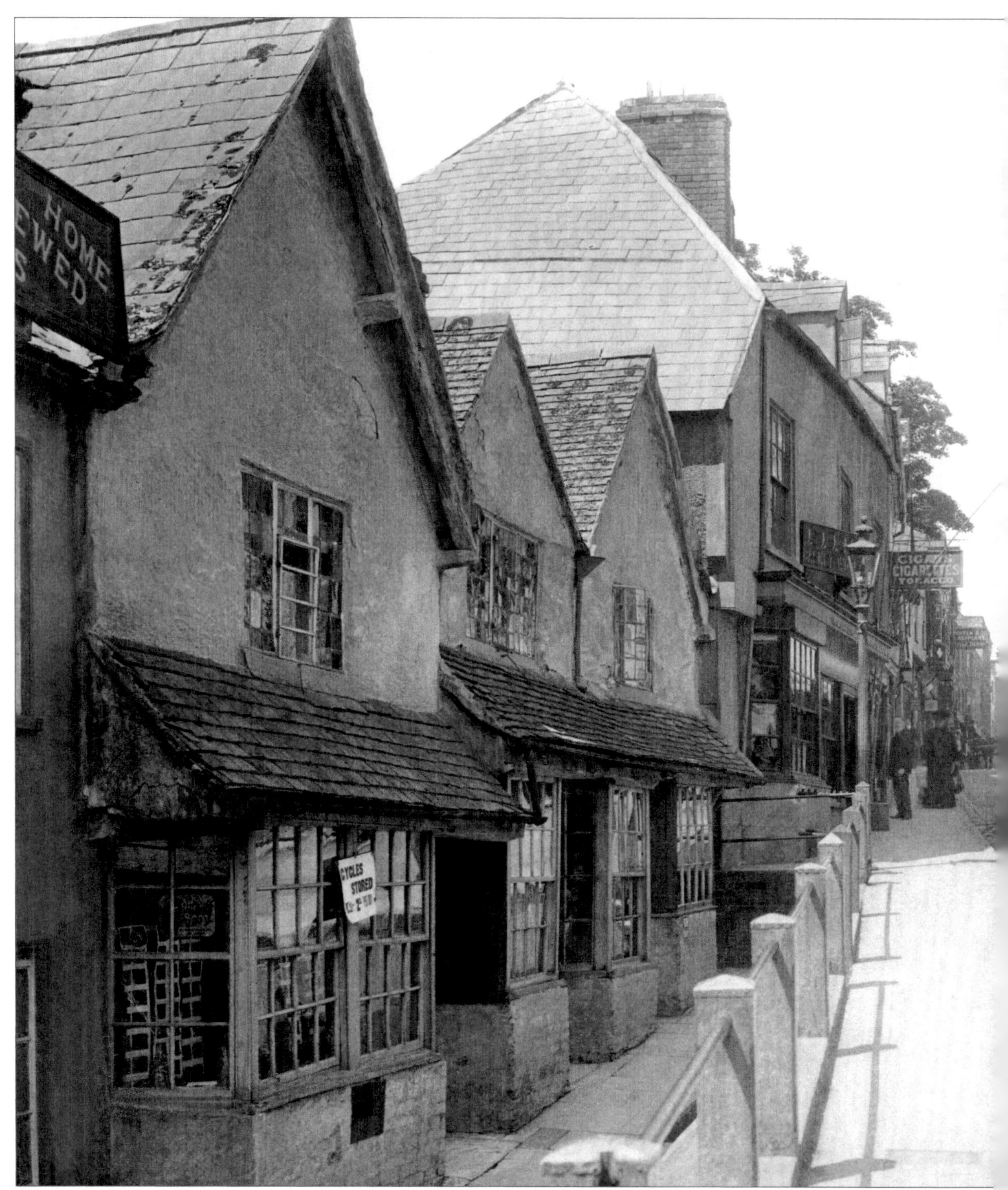
HOME
EWED
S
CYCLES
STORED
CIGARS
CIGARETTES
TOBACCO

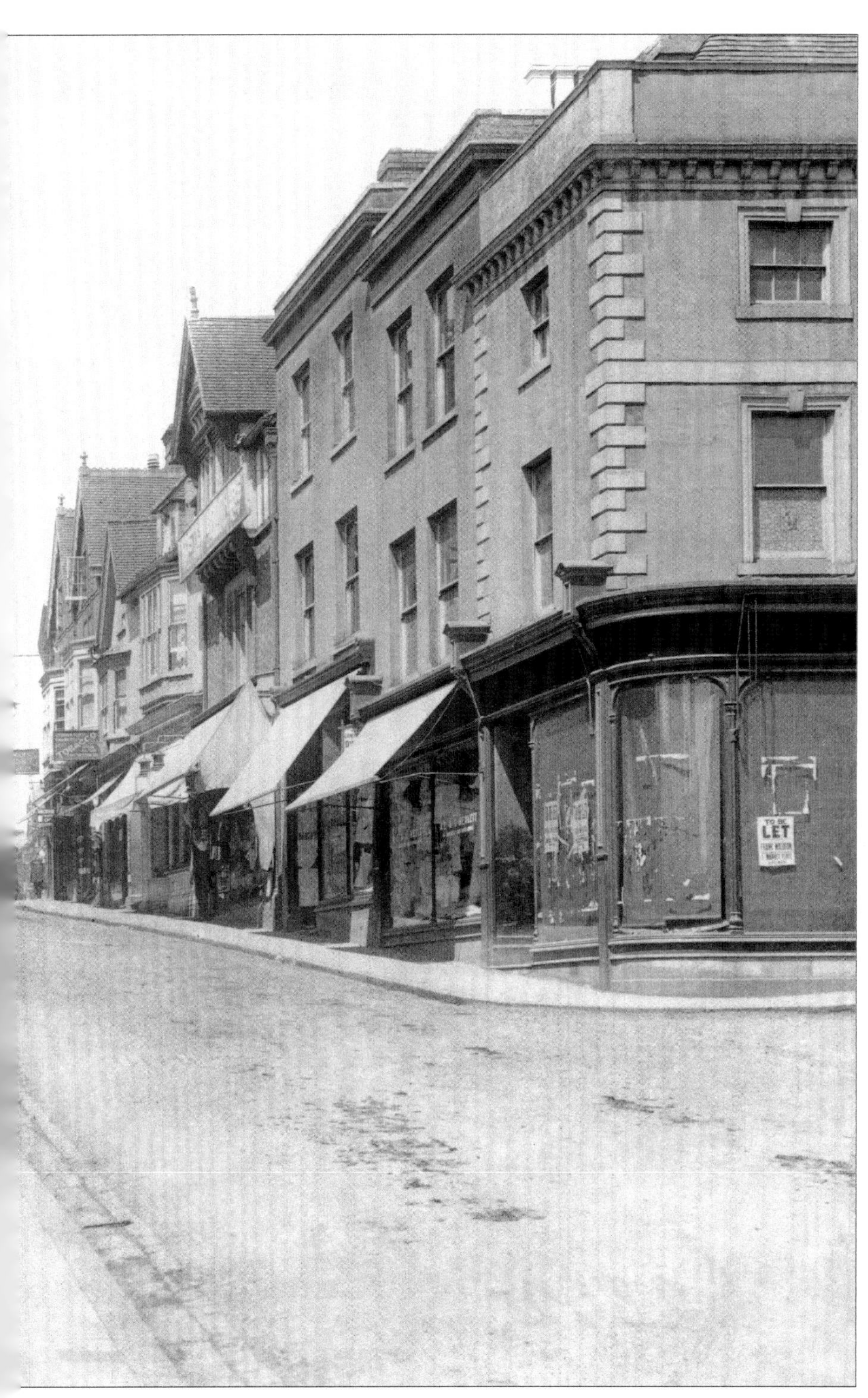

BRIDGE STREET
1910 62352

This scene appears little changed since 1892 (31106, pages 40-41), though the building on the right, at the corner of Bridge Street and Mill Street, has acquired large shop-windows. It was soon to be much more greatly changed, with the loss of part of its upper storey. Today, this entire streetscape has been modernised, with the lovely bays and gables on the left lost altogether.

THE CROWN HOTEL *1893* 32174

Located on the south side of Bridge Street, the Crown Hotel was built in the 16th century as an inn. In coaching days a coach known as the 'Pilot' left the courtyard every day for Warwick. The Crown is no longer an inn or a hotel; today it is occupied by several businesses, most prominent of which is the Crown Tea Rooms. The trees have gone, sad to say.

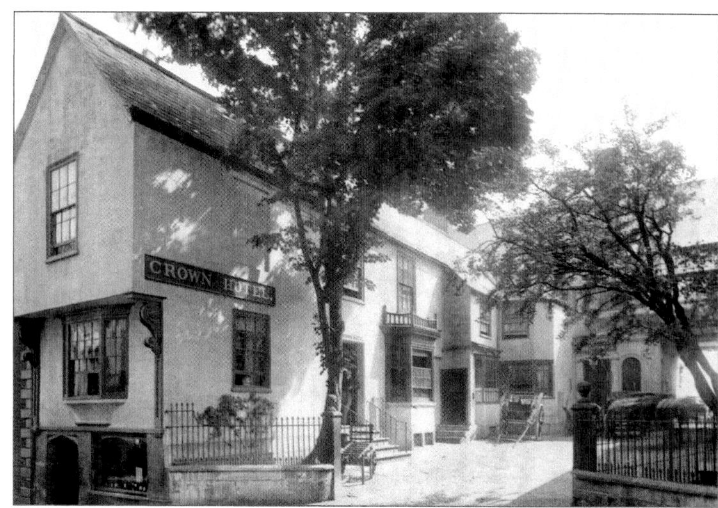

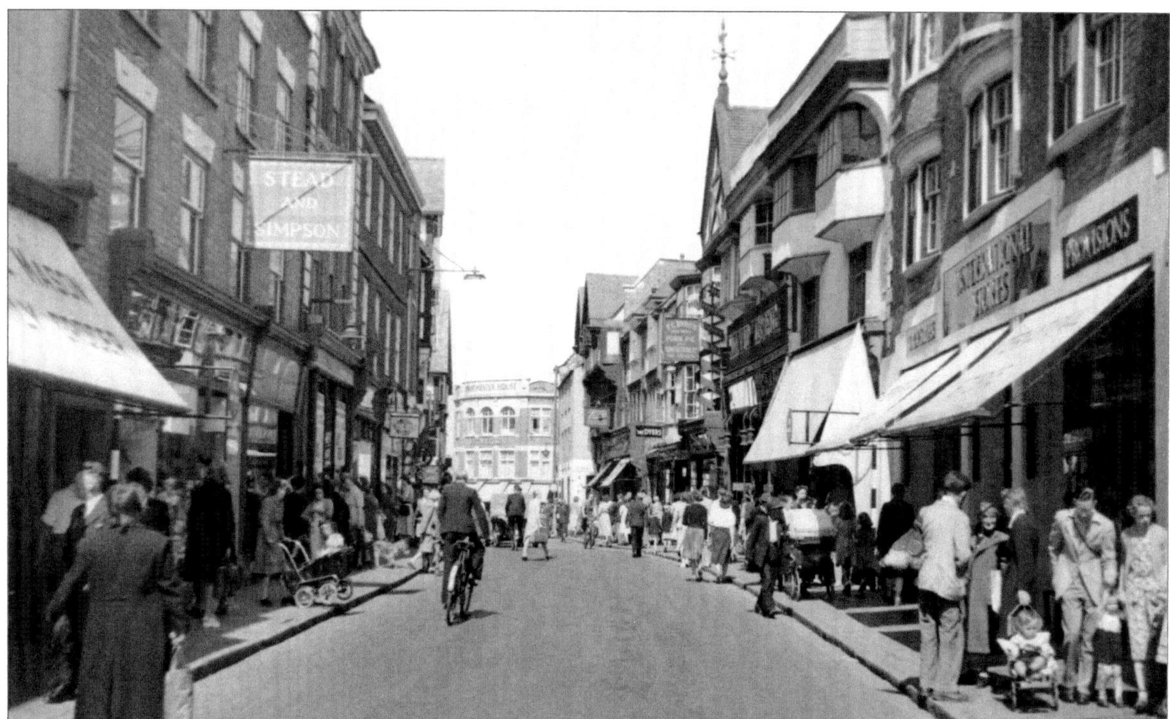

BRIDGE STREET *c1955* E44072

We are looking up Bridge Street, and Manchester House is visible at the top, on High Street. The original Manchester House was a lovely 17th- or 18th-century building (see 31102, page 27) which was demolished for road widening. It was rebuilt to this design in 1931 and now houses an antiques and collectables centre, equipped with a huge CCTV camera pointing down Bridge Street. On the extreme right of this picture is a branch of International Stores, one of the earliest chain stores. The site is now occupied by Boots, which has moved from its earlier location further up the street.

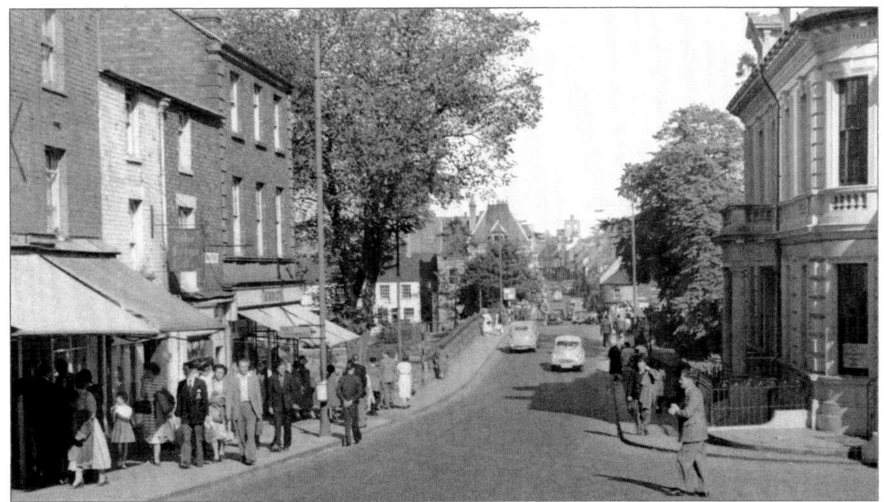

BRIDGE STREET
c1955 E44097

We are looking towards Workman Bridge here, with Port Street and Bengeworth beyond. The word 'port' used to mean market, and it was in 1055 that Edward the Confessor declared Evesham a port. The imposing building on the right is unchanged today, but those across the road have suffered from the poor-quality modernisation of the left-hand one, which has spoilt the whole block.

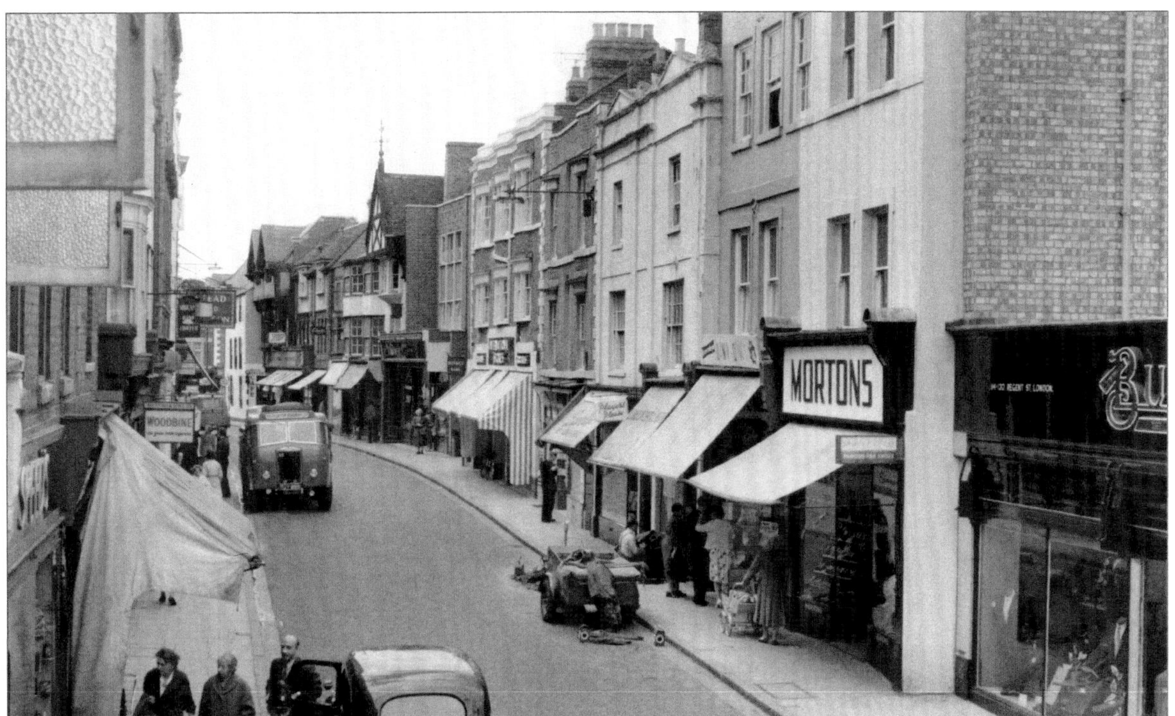

BRIDGE STREET *c1960* E44116

International Stores (see E44072 opposite), in the centre of this picture, on the right, is now occupied by Boots, and fortunately its superb curvy upper storeys are intact. The building to the right of it also remains unspoiled, but the next two have been horribly rebuilt. To the left of International Stores stands one of the first examples of post-war change in Bridge Street. This building replaced a much older one some time in the late 1950s. To its left, the building with a timbered gable is Langstone House, where Charles I stayed in 1644. To the left again, the twin-gabled building was occupied by Boots in 1960.

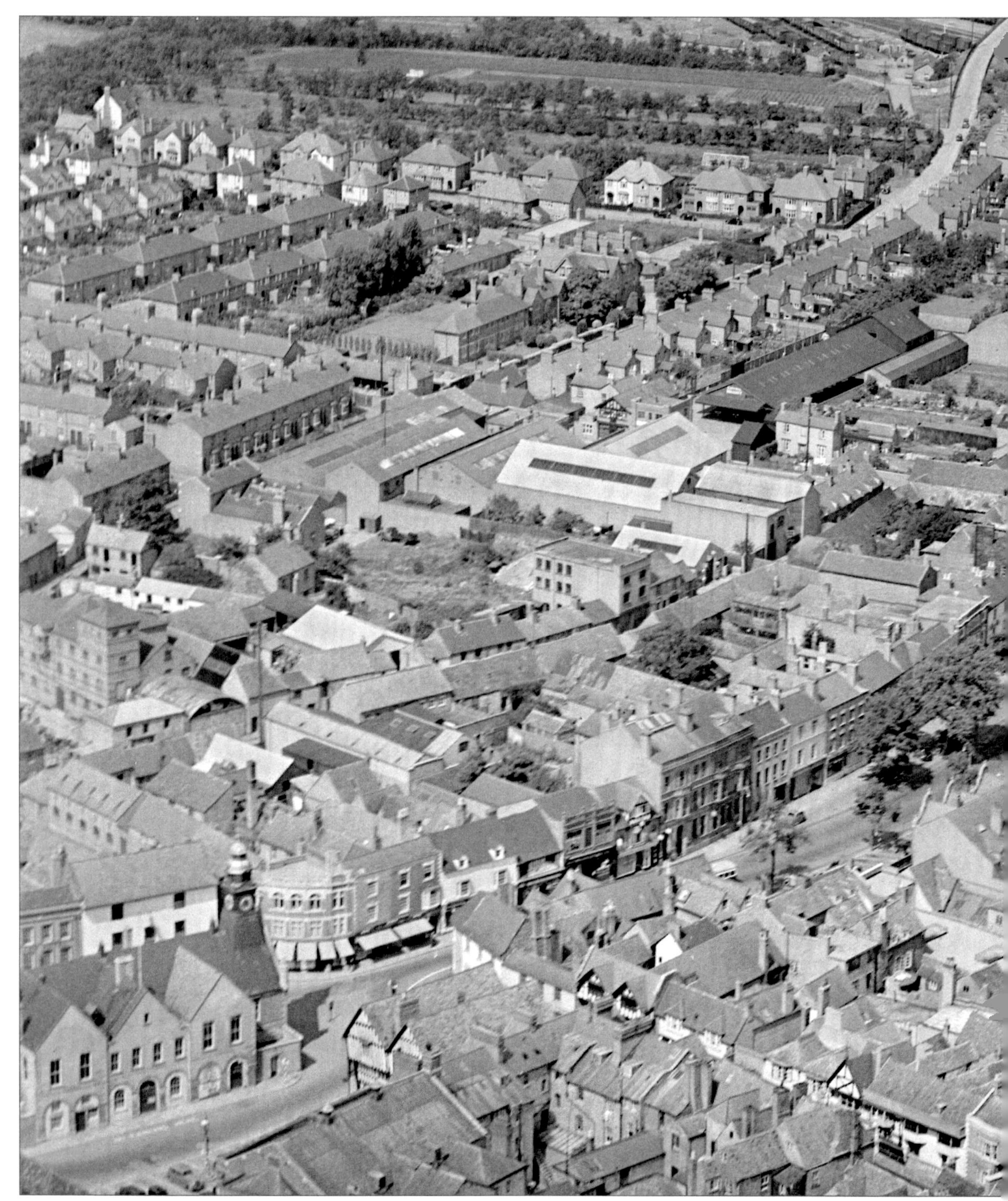

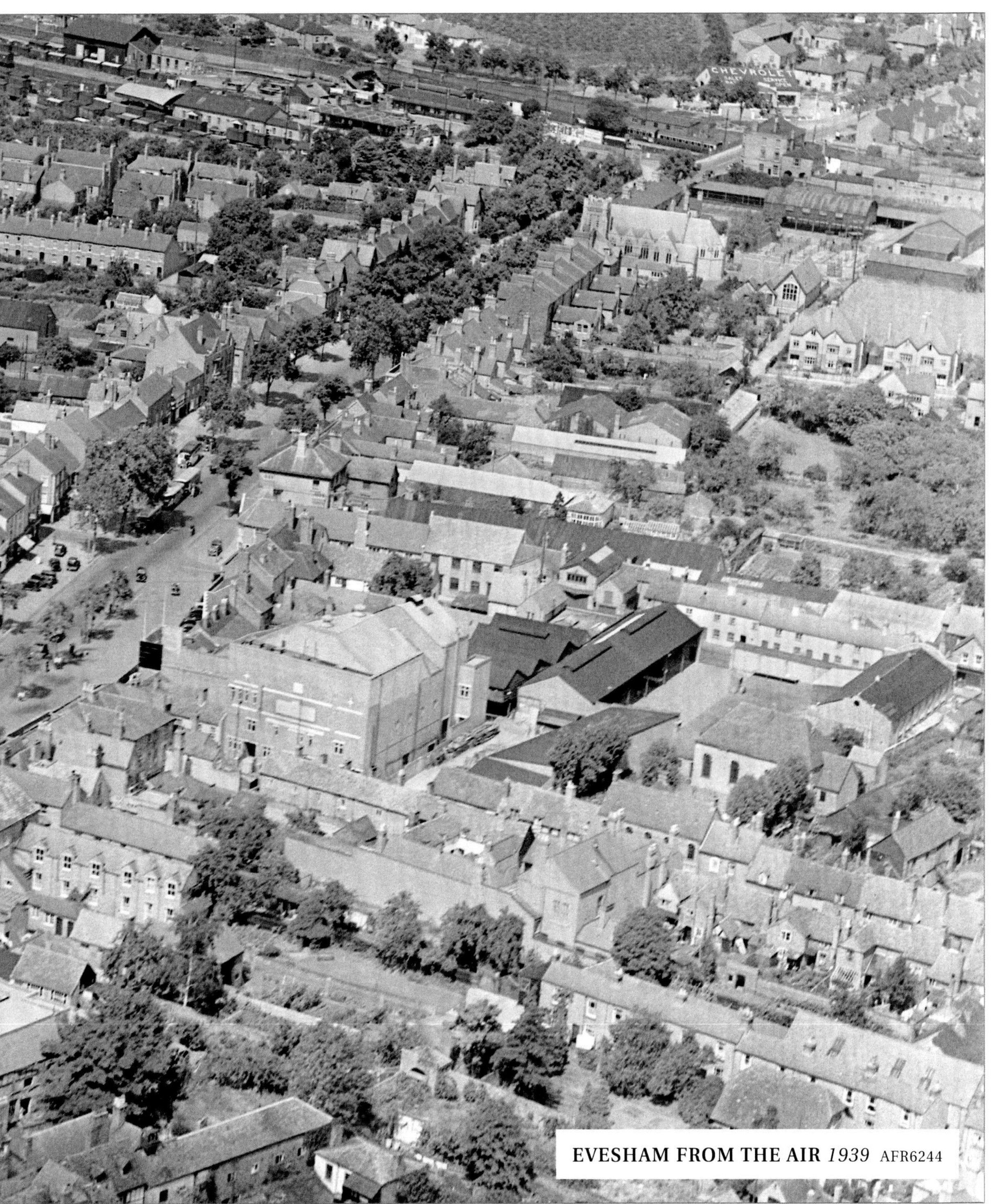

EVESHAM FROM THE AIR *1939* AFR6244

THE WAR MEMORIAL AND THE BELL TOWER *1922* 72432

Abbey Park's war memorial, which occupies the centre ground in this scene, was built to the memory of the men of Evesham who fell in the 'Great War 1914-20'. The unexpected date is explained by the fact that the Worcestershire Regiment fought in Russia, where peace was not declared until 1920. The names of those who died in the Second World War have since been added too.

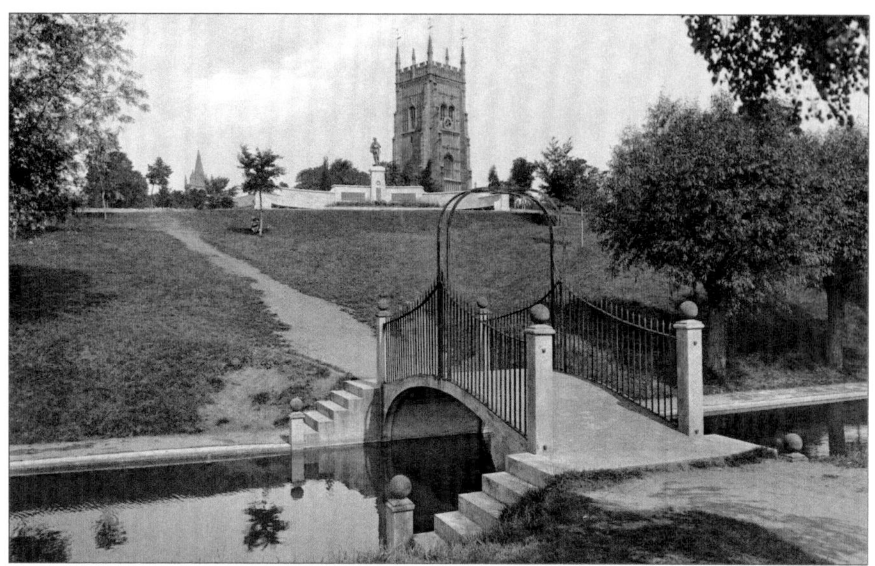

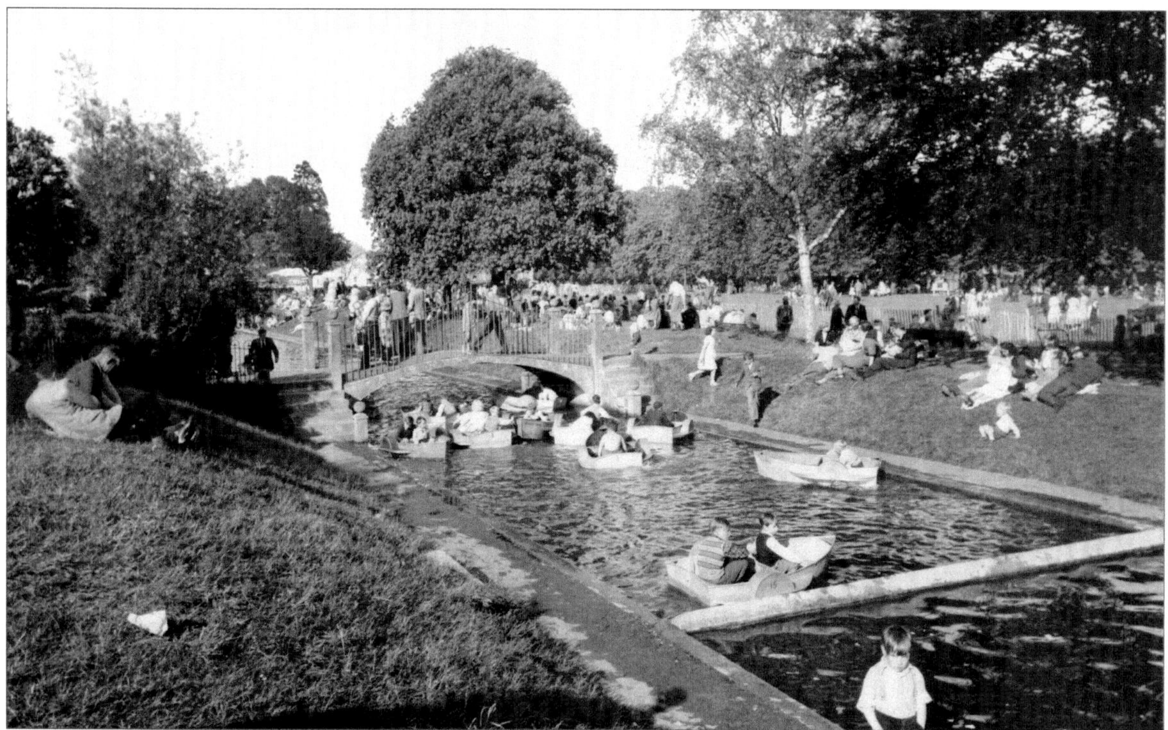

THE CHILDREN'S BOATING POOL, *Abbey Park c1955* E44085

In medieval times this was a fish pool used by the monks. By the 1920s it had become a formal pool, but in the 1950s it was made into a children's boating pool. This later fell into disuse, and in 2002 part of it was converted into ornamental gardens. However, some water has been retained, and children can at least play with model boats.

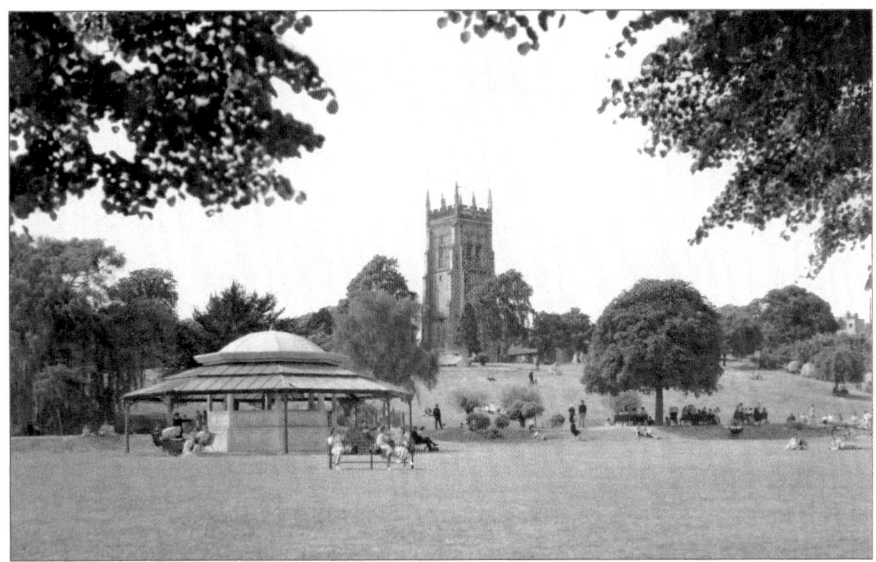

THE BANDSTAND
Abbey Park
c1955 E44066

Abbey Park was awarded a Green Flag by the Civic Trust in 2005 for achieving a 'national standard of excellence'. It has extensive riverside meadows, a superb lime avenue, and a variety of facilities. Numerous events are held in the meadows throughout the year. The bandstand has lost the wide-spreading canopy but continues in use, with a different band playing here each summer Sunday afternoon.

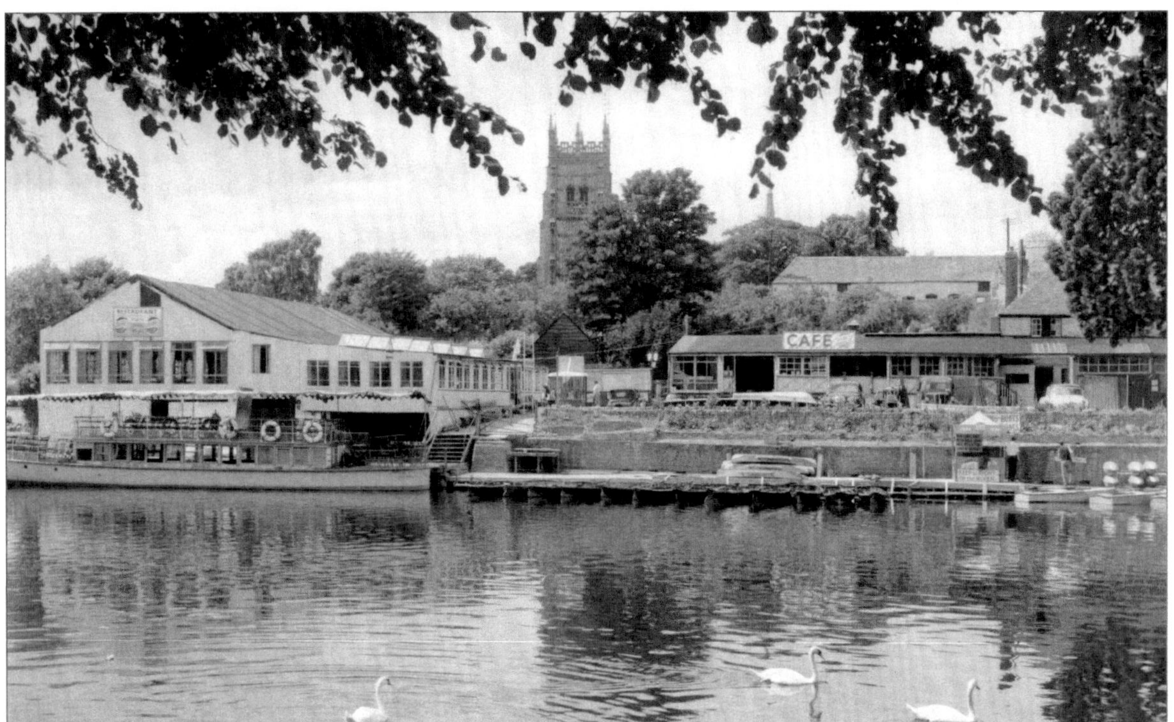

THE RIVER AVON *c1960* E44114

The photographer must have been standing close to Workman Bridge to take this picture. All of this clutter has gone now, but the bell tower has to share the scene with new clutter in the form of riverside apartment blocks and a multi-storey car park attached to Riverside Shopping Centre.

▶ THE BELL TOWER FROM THE AVON
1892 31088

This small building still stands, but has been incorporated into a much larger one. It is used by Evesham Rowing Club, which was founded in 1863 as Evesham Boat Club with the intention of holding a regatta to coincide with the agricultural and horticultural shows in September. The club's boathouse was just a wooden shed at that time, but it moved into this building c1890. The regatta was successful and became an annual event. The principal prize was the Vale of Evesham Challenge Trophy, a silver model of the Bell Tower. It was stolen in 1966 and never recovered.

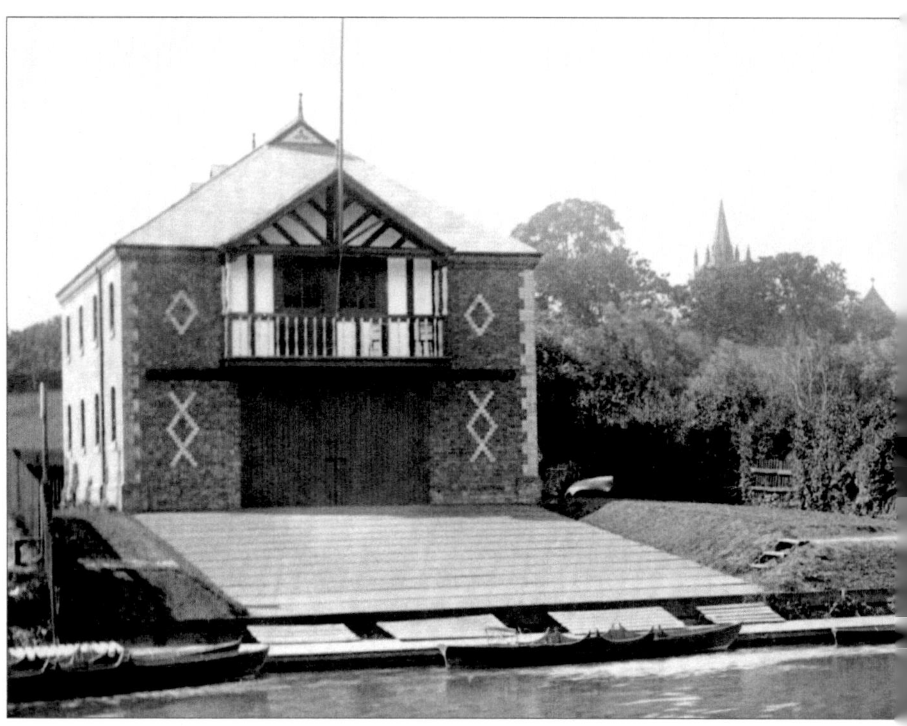

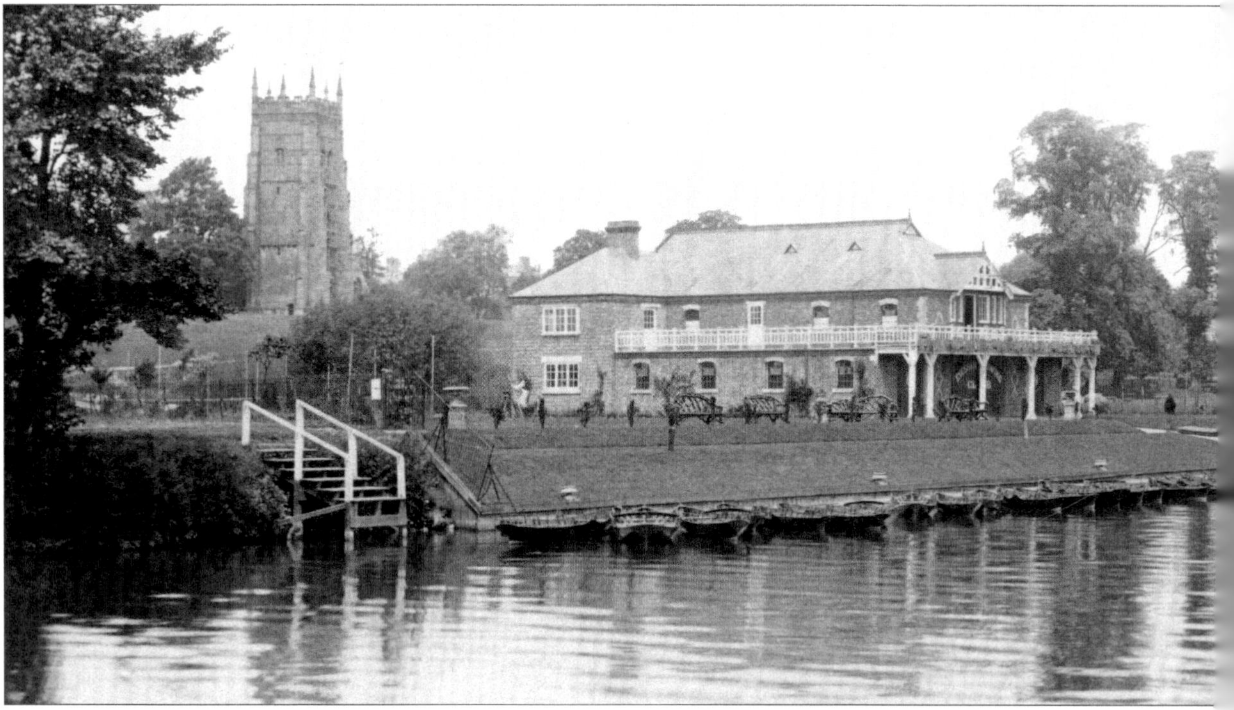

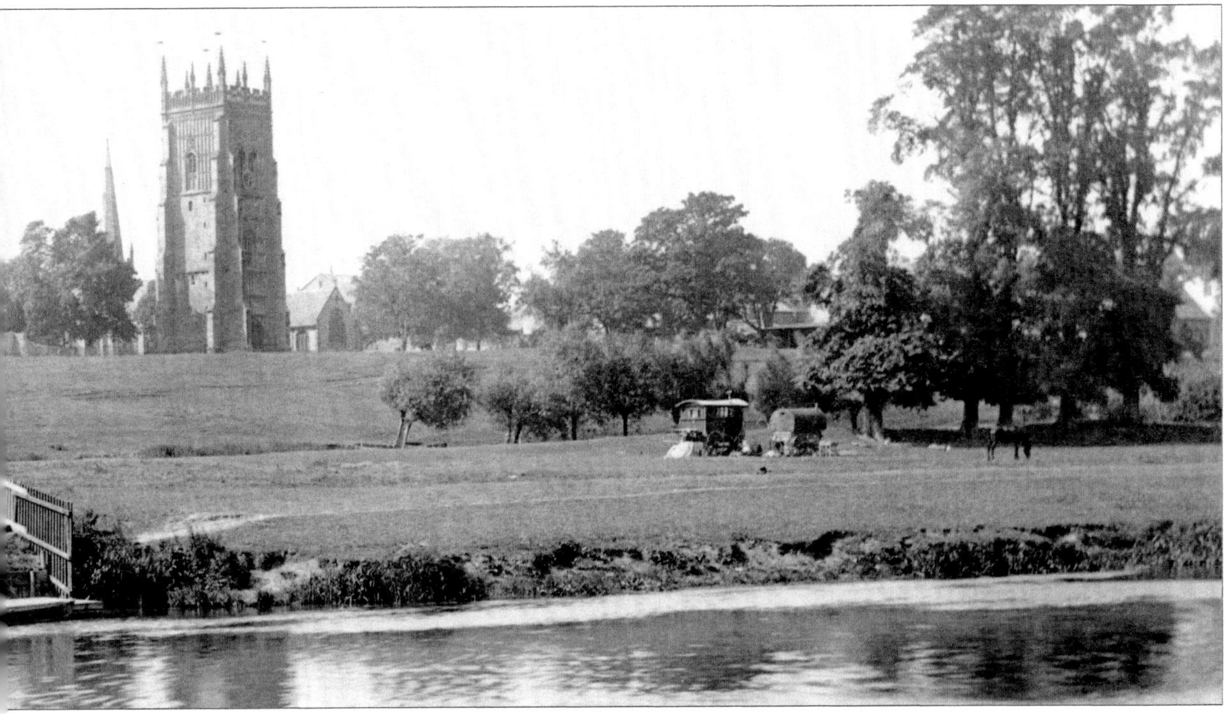

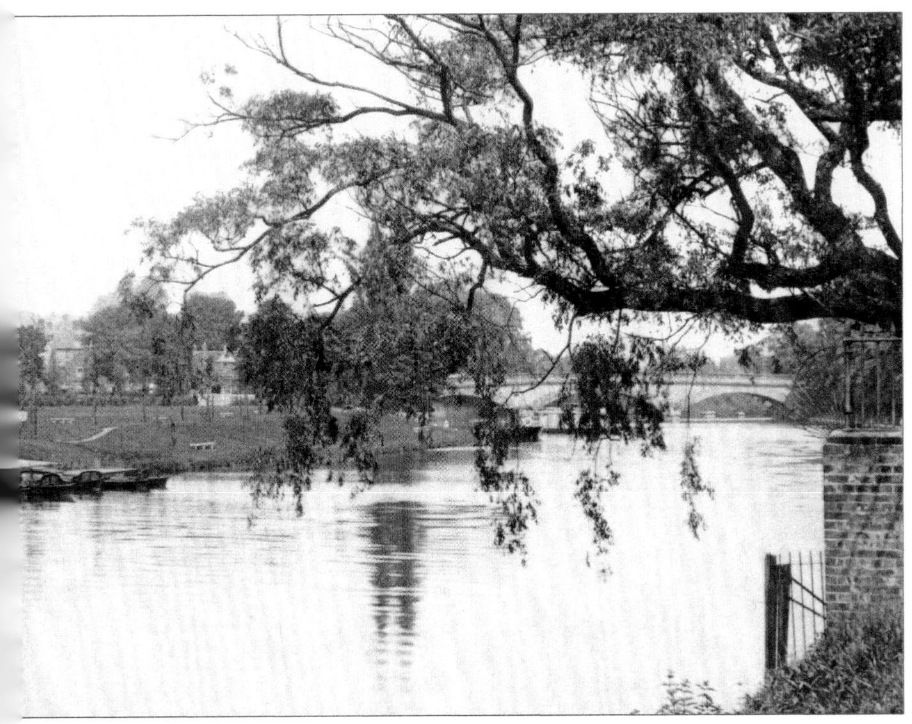

THE RIVER AND THE BOATHOUSE *1910* 62330

The small boathouse seen in 31088 (above) was soon extended to form this structure, which has itself since been extended. Evesham makes the most of the Avon, with high-quality riverside green space, boat hire, boat trips, visitors' moorings and angling festivals. Evesham Regatta takes place in May, Evesham River Festival in July, and the Head of the River Regatta in August.

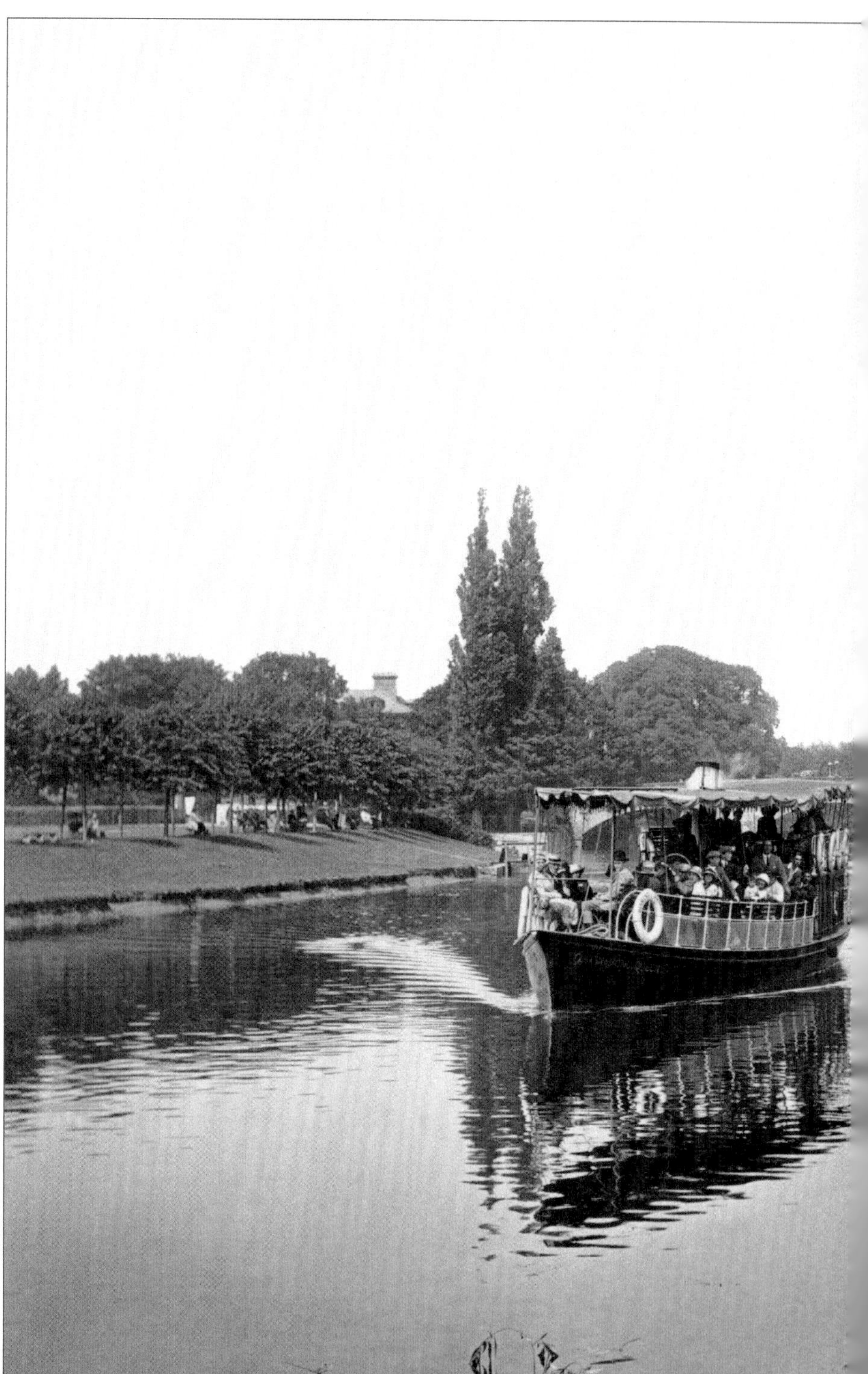

THE RIVER AND THE BRIDGE *1922* 72428

This area is still open to the public and is known as Workman Gardens. In the background is Workman Bridge, built in the 1850s to replace the old Evesham Bridge. A plaque on the bridge records the 'public spirit and perseverance' of Henry Workman, the solicitor who lobbied for a new bridge and helped raise funds for it. Evesham was grateful enough to elect him mayor five times. The gardens were created soon after the bridge was completed. The crowded pleasure steamer reflects the popularity of the river, something which endures to this day, despite the abundance of competing attractions.

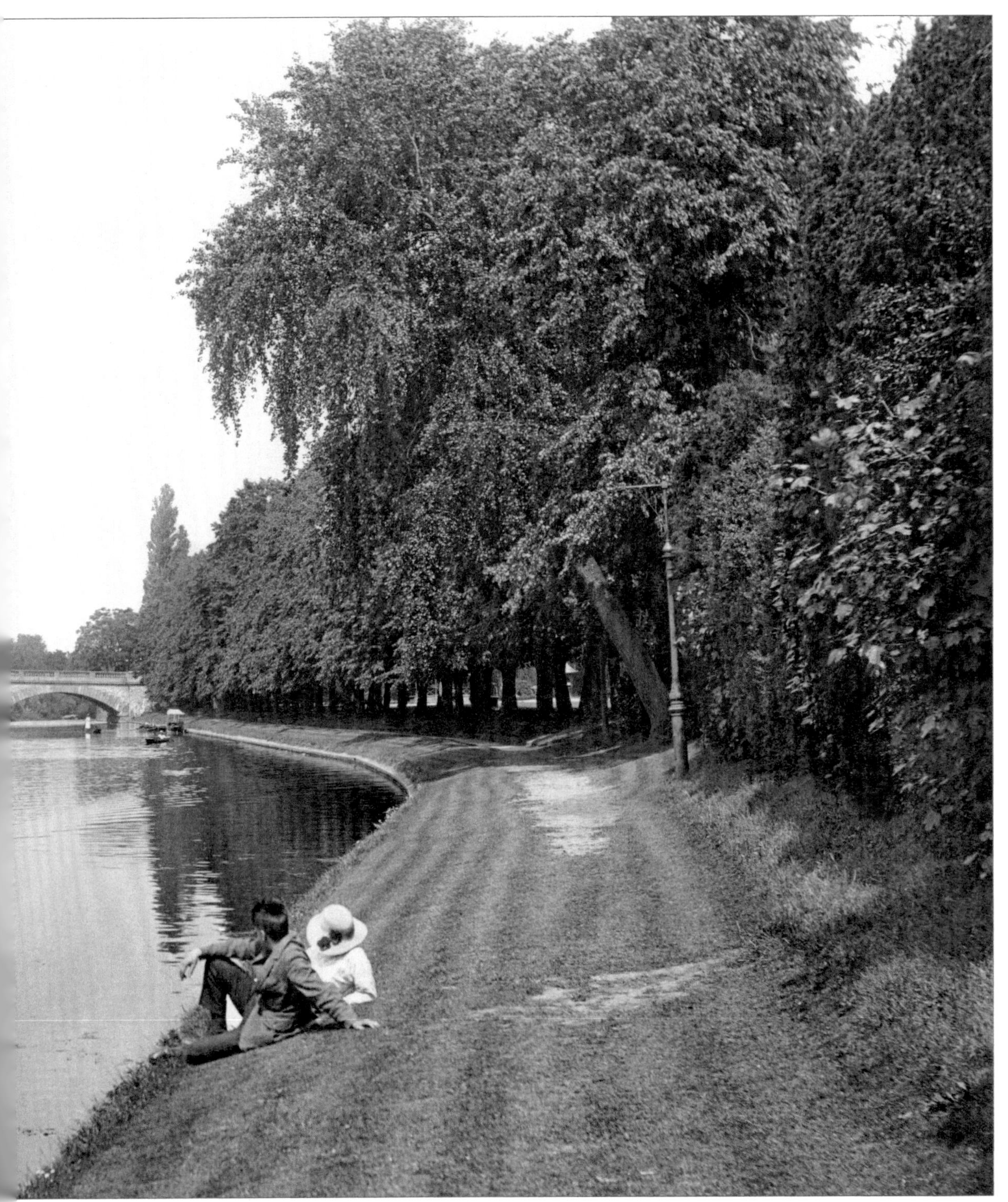

▶ THE RIVER AND THE BRIDGE *c1955* E44079

New Bridge, also known as Abbey Bridge, was built of pre-stressed reinforced Feathercrete concrete and opened in 1928. Its purpose was to provide a shorter route into town and to take traffic from Workman Bridge. It has now acquired a constant flow of vehicles, a set of traffic lights and the tired, scruffy look common to most concrete structures more than a few years old.

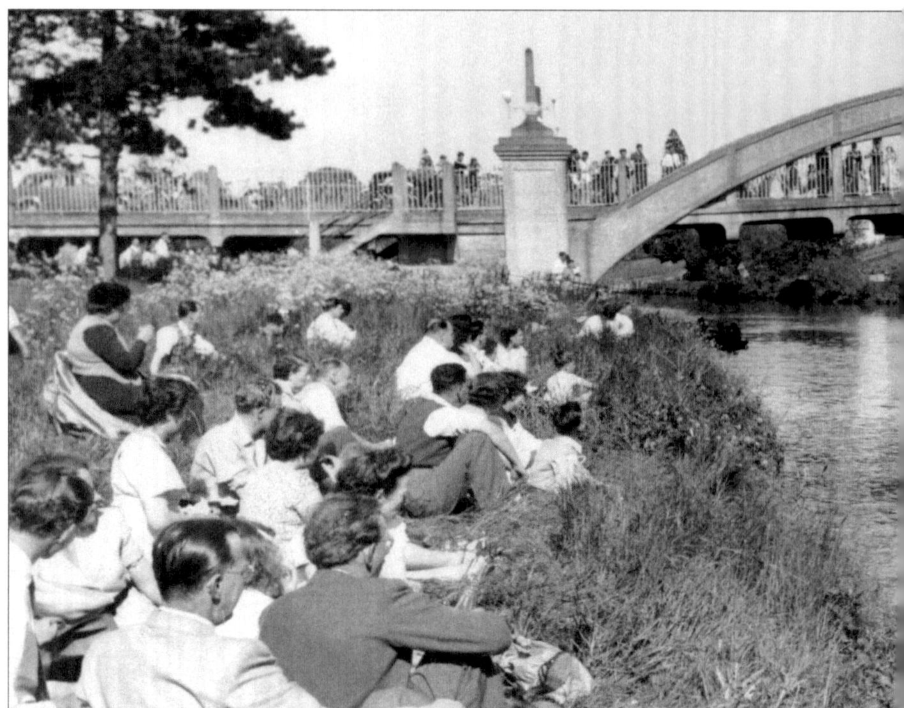

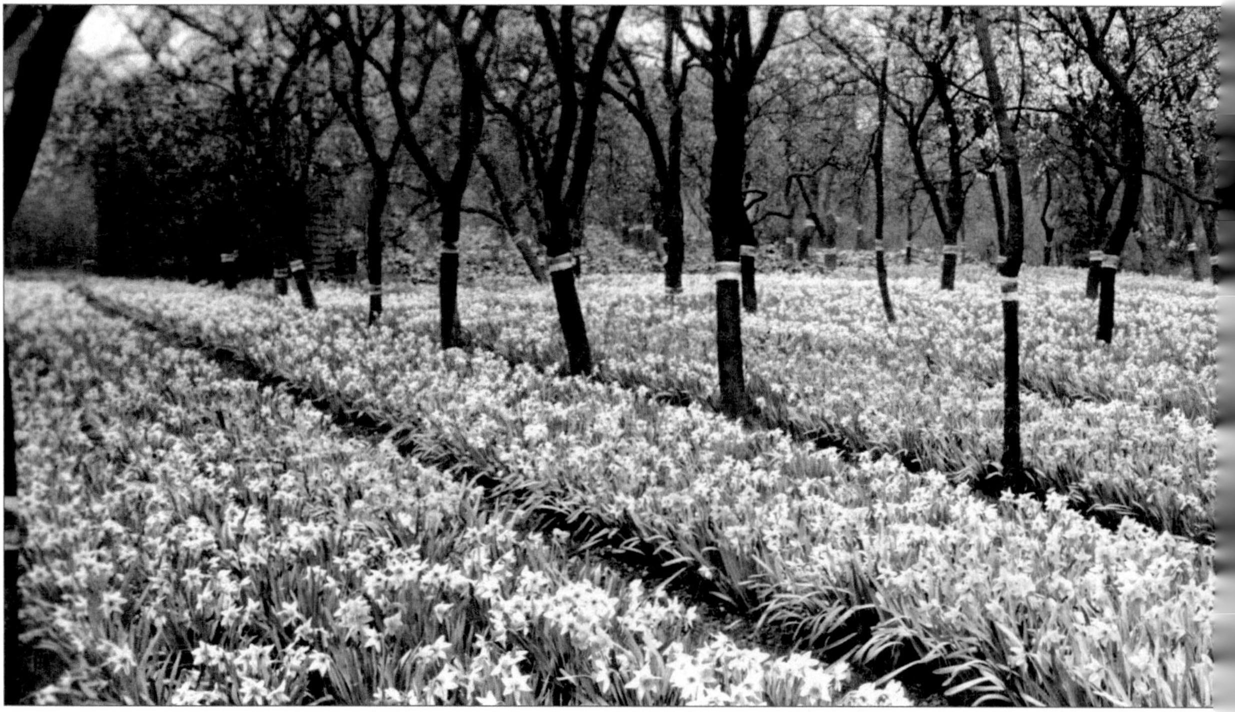

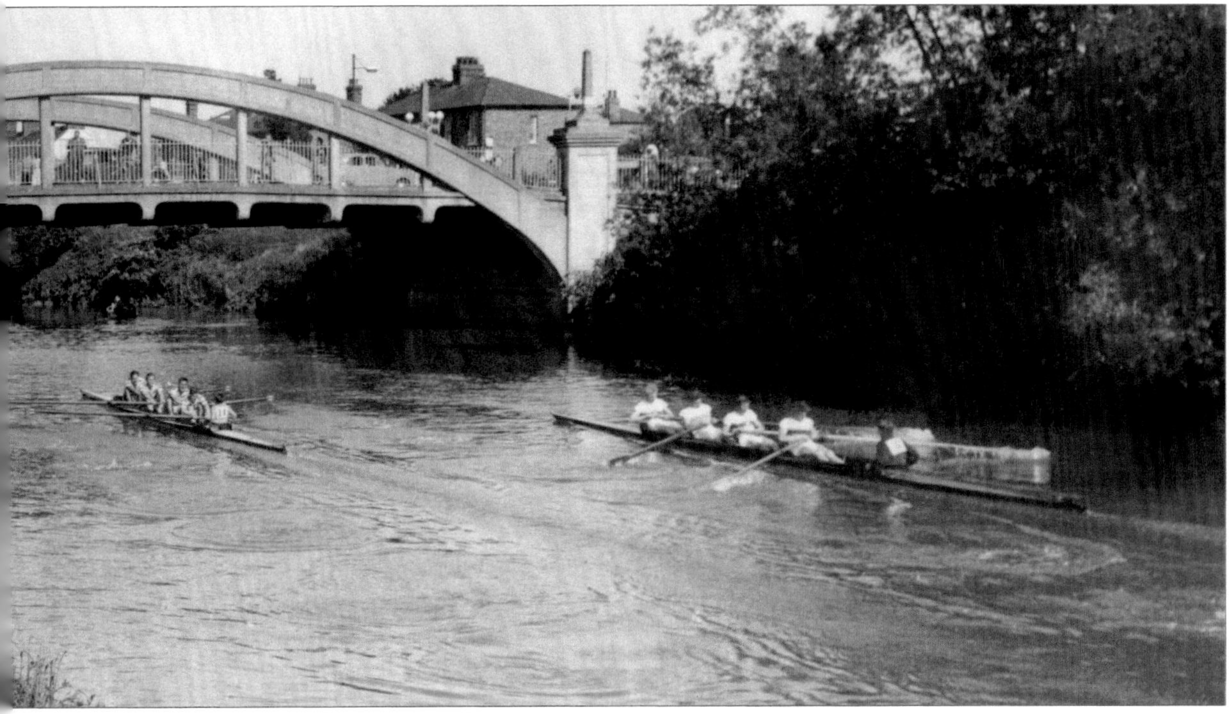

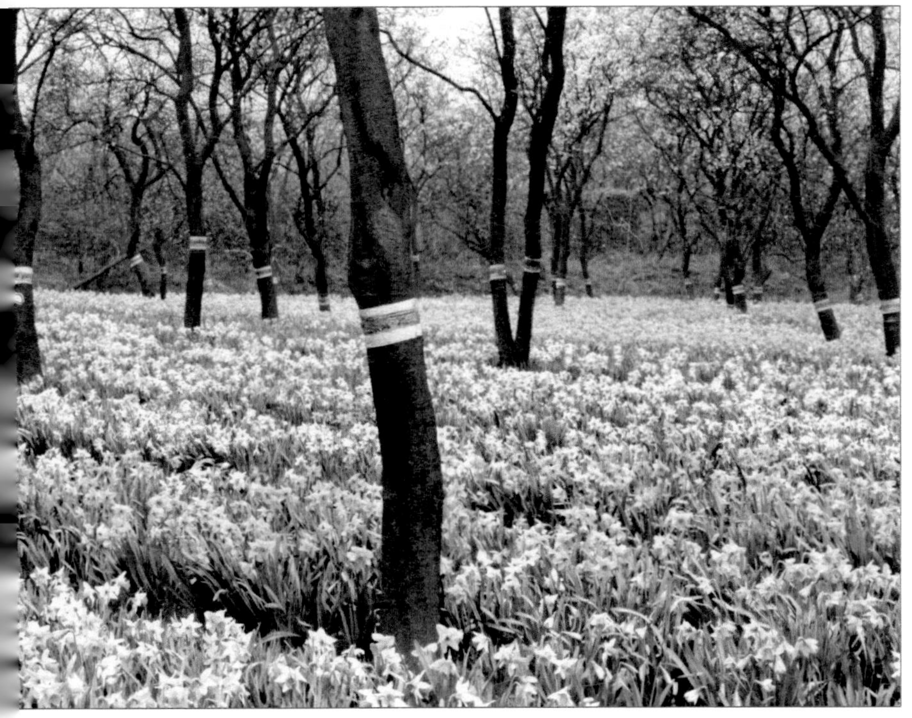

◄ DAFFODILS
c1955 E44049

Flower growing became important in Evesham in the late 19th century, helped by the railways and by increasing prosperity which allowed the purchase of small luxuries. The flowers were usually grown under fruit trees in orchards. These daffodils could be anywhere - even today there are still orchards in Evesham - but are most likely to have been growing in the riverside orchards near Hampton Ferry.

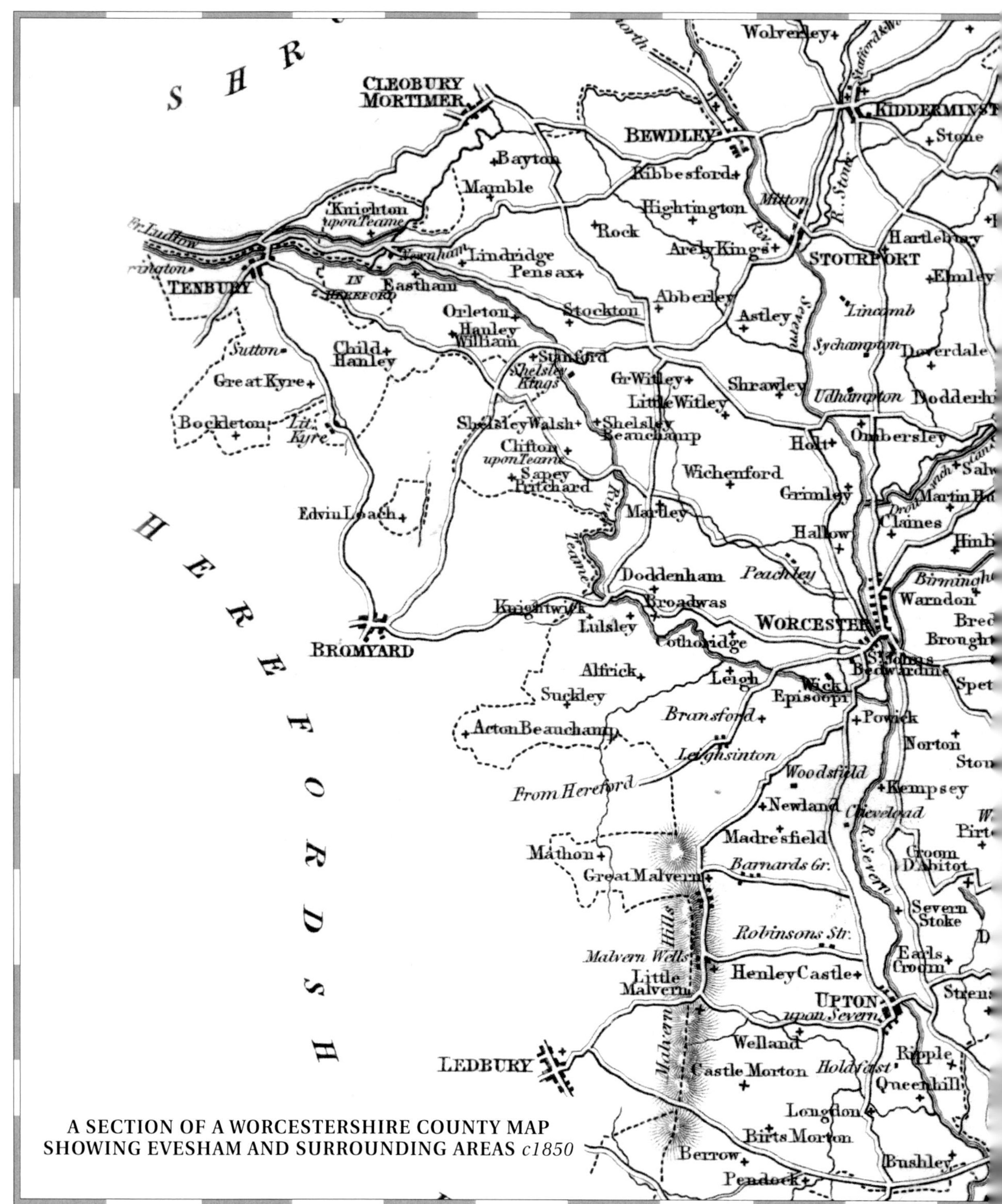

A SECTION OF A WORCESTERSHIRE COUNTY MAP SHOWING EVESHAM AND SURROUNDING AREAS *c1850*

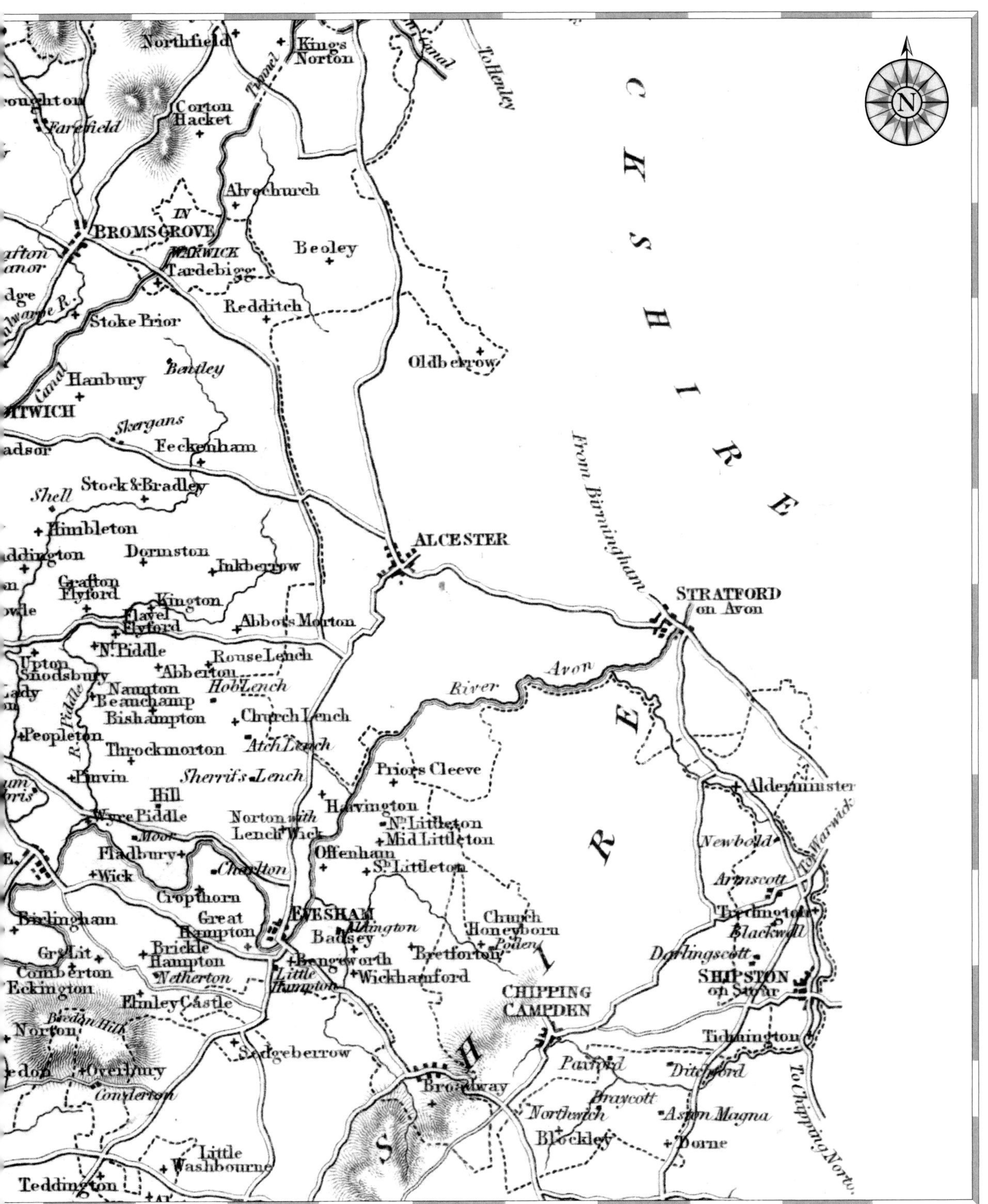
WARWICKSHIRE
To Henley
Tunnel
Canal
From Birmingham
To Warwick
To Chipping Norton
Northfield
Kings Norton
Corton Hacket
Farefield
oughton
Alvechurch
Beoley
BROMSGROVE
IN WARWICK
Tardebigg
afton anor
dge
Stoke Prior
Redditch
Oldberrow
Hanbury
Bentley
ITWICH
adsor
Skergans
Feckenham
Shell
Stock & Bradley
ALCESTER
Himbleton
ddington
Dormston
Inkberrow
Grafton Flyford
Kington
Flavel Flyford
Abbots Morton
STRATFORD on Avon
Upton Snodsbury
N. Piddle
Rouse Lench
Abberton
Hob Lench
River
Avon
ady
Naunton Beauchamp
Church Lench
R. Piddle
Bishampton
Peopleton
Throckmorton
Atch Lench
Alderminster
Pinvin
Sherrif's Lench
Priors Cleeve
an ris
Hill
Havington
Newbold
Wyre Piddle
Norton with Lench Wick
N. Littleton
Arnscott
Moor
Mid Littleton
Fladbury
Offenham
Charlton
St. Littleton
Turchington
Wick
Blackwell
Cropthorn
EVESHAM
Church Honeyborn
Darlingscott
Birlingham
Great Hampton
Aldington
Badsey
Pollen
SHIPSTON on Savar
Gr. Lit
Brickle Hampton
Bengeworth
Bretforton
Comberton
Netherton
Wickhamford
Eckington
Little Hampton
Tidmington
Elmley Castle
CHIPPING CAMPDEN
Bredon Hill
Norton
Pavford
Ditchford
edon
Overbury
Comberton
Sedgeberrow
Broadway
Northwich
Braycott
Aston Magna
Little Washbourne
Blockley
Dorne
Teddington

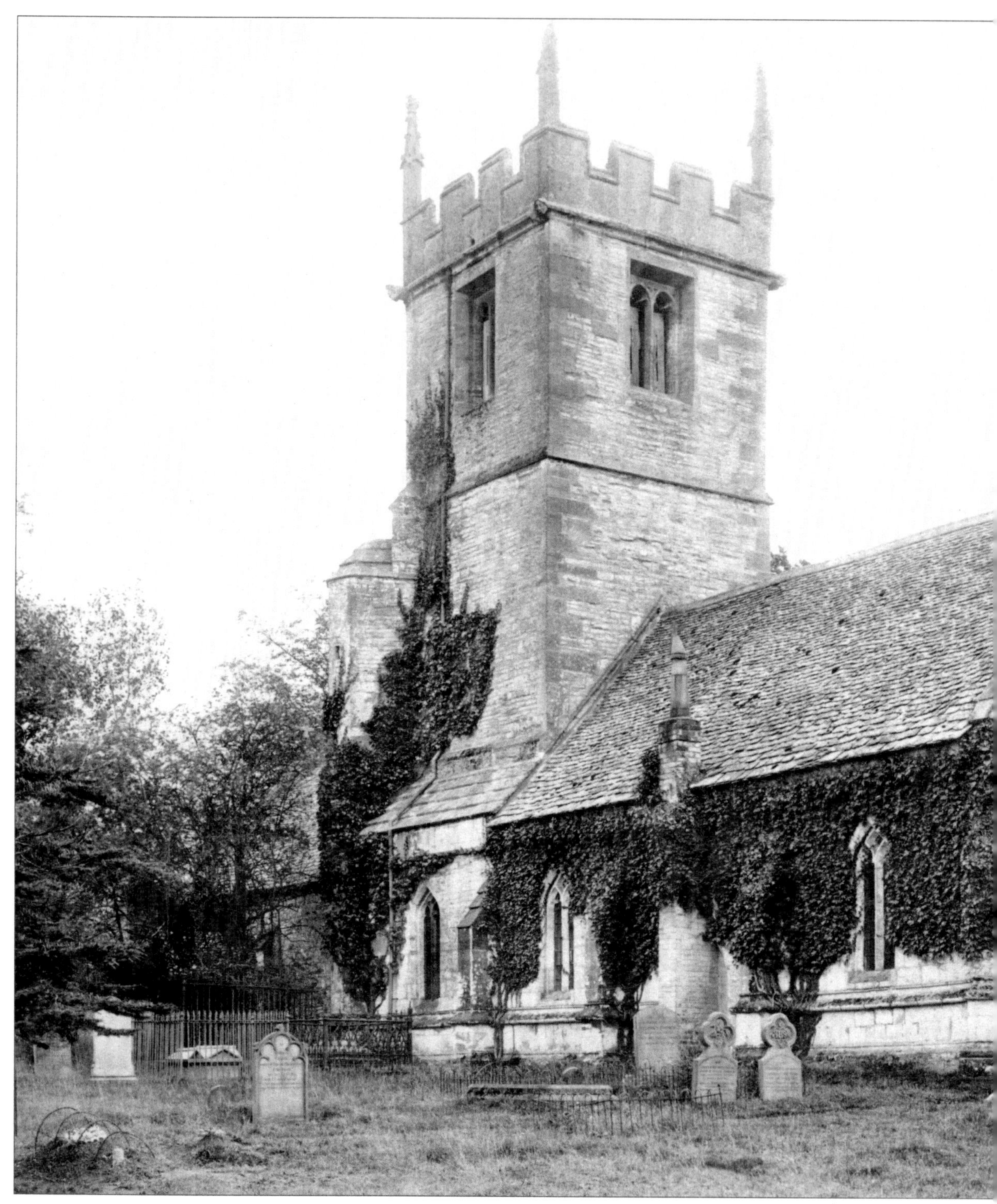

DOWNSTREAM FROM EVESHAM

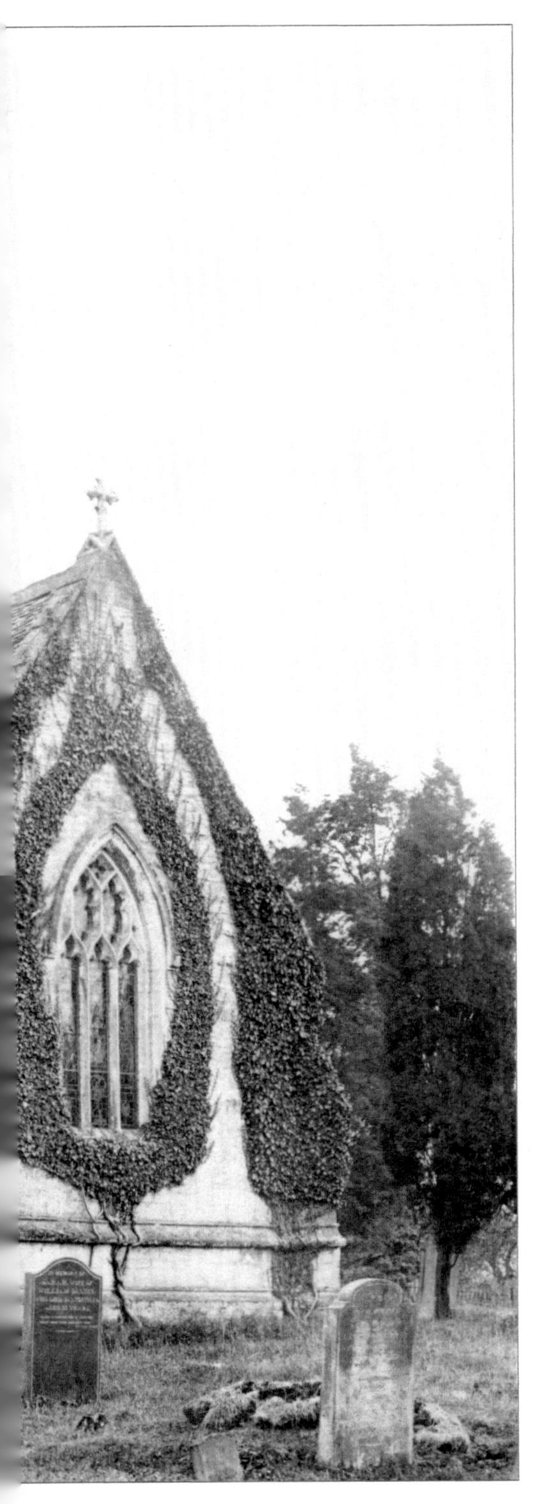

HAMPTON, *St Andrew's Church 1895* 36970

Once a settlement in its own right, Hampton is now a suburb of
Evesham, located on the other side of the Avon. St Andrew's is a most
attractive building surrounded by a flower-filled churchyard, which
is at its best in March when primroses, lesser celandine, violets and
daffodils bloom. There are some fine headstones as well as the superb
tomb of John Martin, who died in 1714.

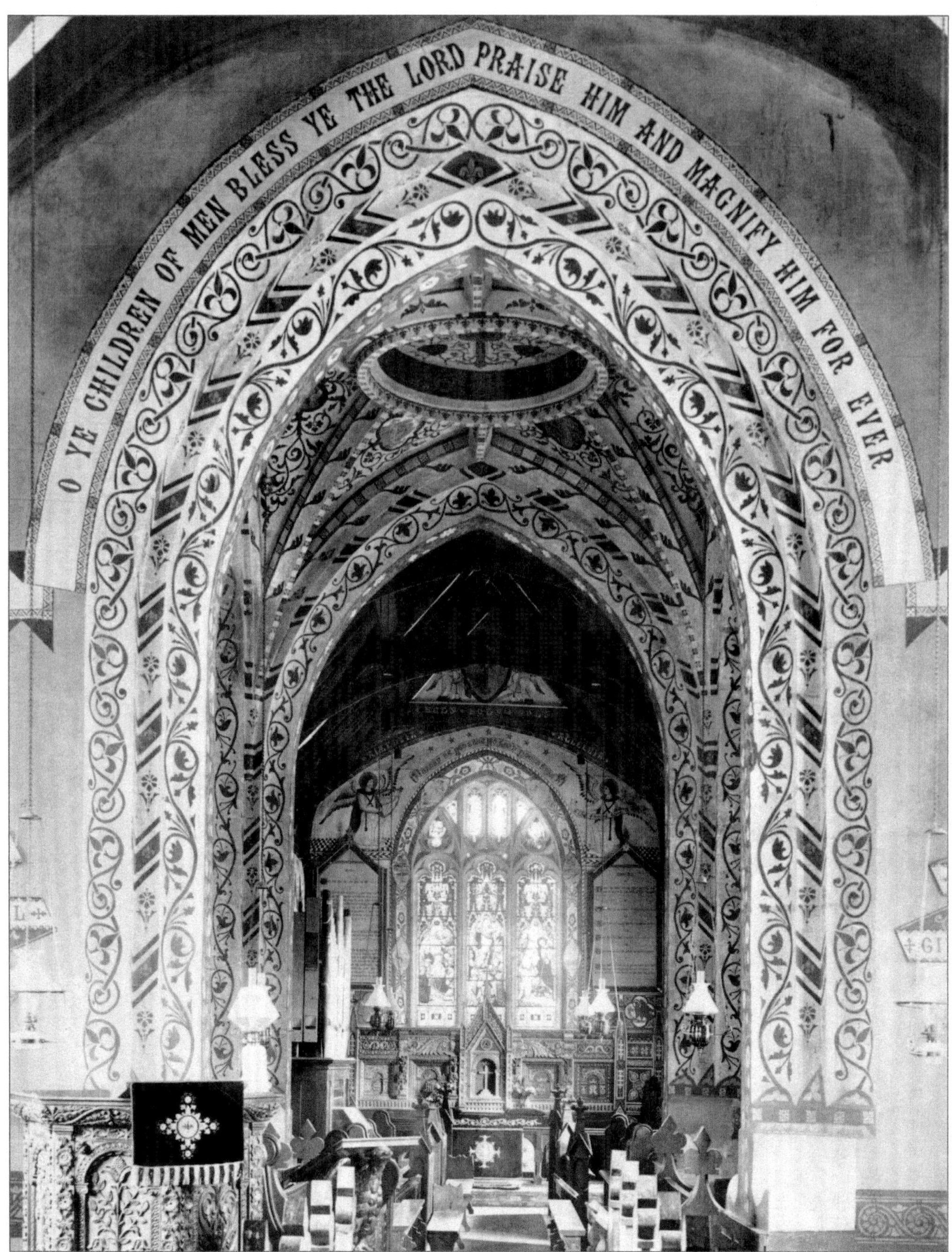

HAMPTON, *St Andrew's Church, the Interior 1895* 36972

Believed to be Norman in origin, St Andrew's was rebuilt in 1282 and enlarged in the 15th century. Some Norman architectural fragments have been re-set in the nave walls. In its structural plan it is unlike other churches of the vale in that it has a central tower.

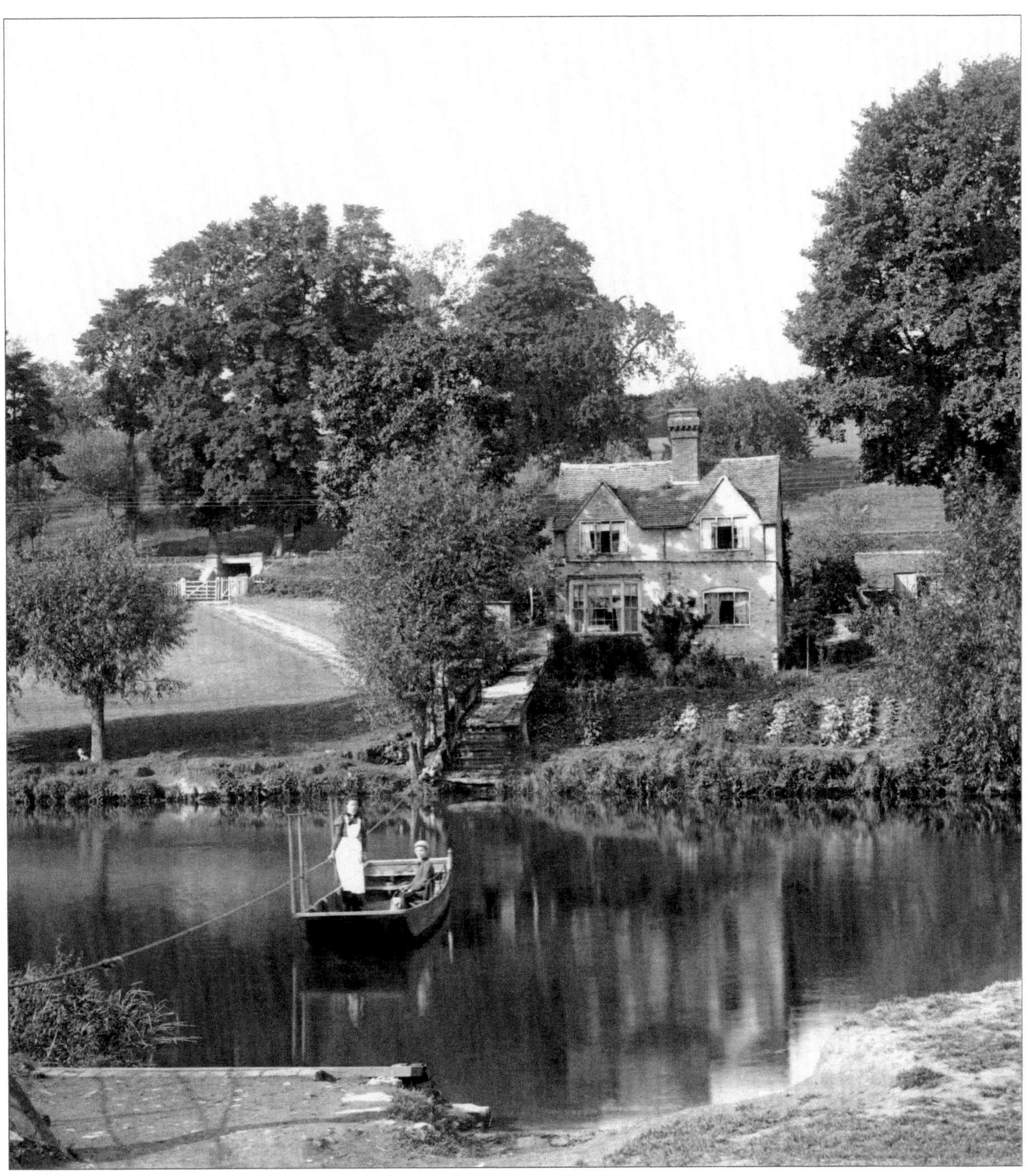

HAMPTON FERRY *1895* 36969

A short walk through riverside meadows, or along Boat Lane from Merstow Green, leads to Hampton Ferry. Believed to have been first operated by the monks, this may be England's oldest chain ferry. It still operates in the summer, linking Evesham with Hampton. At the time of this photo the return fare was one halfpenny. It is now one pound.

FROM CLARK'S HILL
1895 36954

Behind Hampton Ferry is the rising ground known now as Clark's Hill, but originally Clerk's Hill (because of its association with the monks). It shows signs of past terracing, evidence that this is where the monks cultivated their vineyard. The view of Evesham from the hill is not greatly changed, though the orchards have mostly gone. Nonetheless, there is still agricultural land, though much of it is now covered by glasshouses. There is parkland too, and sports fields, though industrial units and new housing also make their presence felt. Clark's Hill itself is mainly grassland and scrub, with remnant orchards.

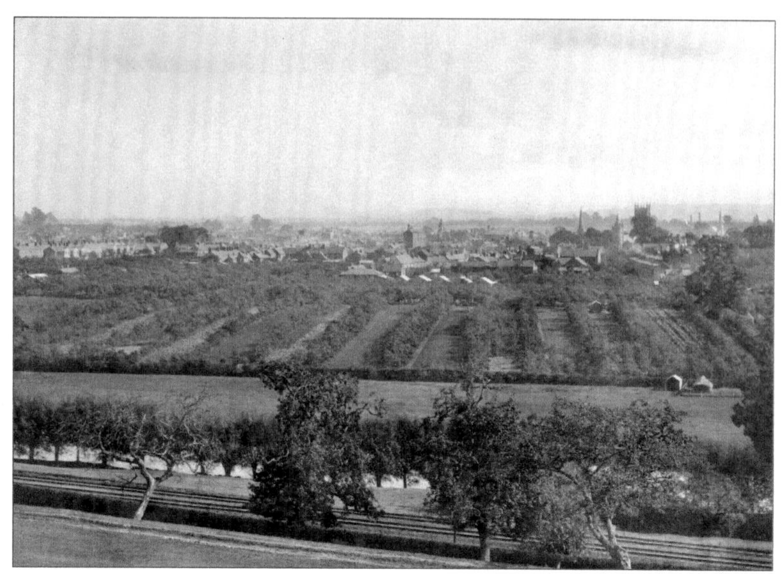

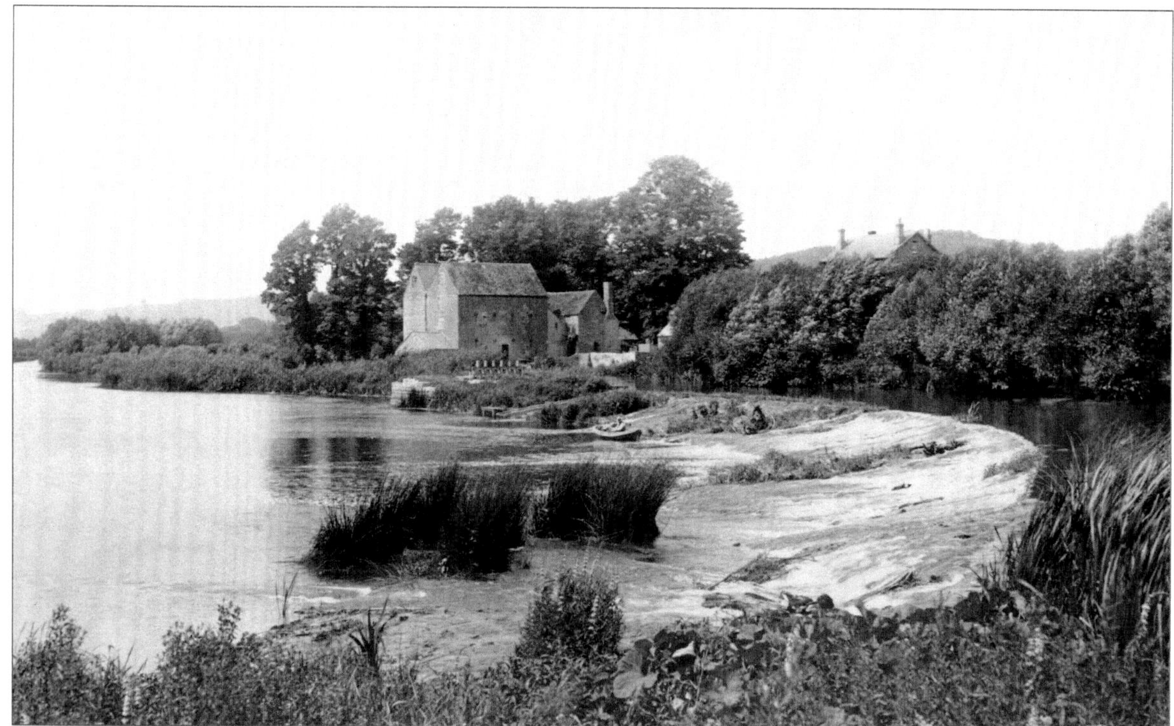

CHADBURY MILL *1899* 44120

The mill was restored 1952-53, but has been converted into a house. It stands by Chadbury Lock, which was the first to be rebuilt by the Lower Avon Navigation Trust in 1952-53, with the help of the Royal Engineers. It was restored again in 2005. Chadbury Weir was restored in the 1990s, when eel and elver passes were also created.

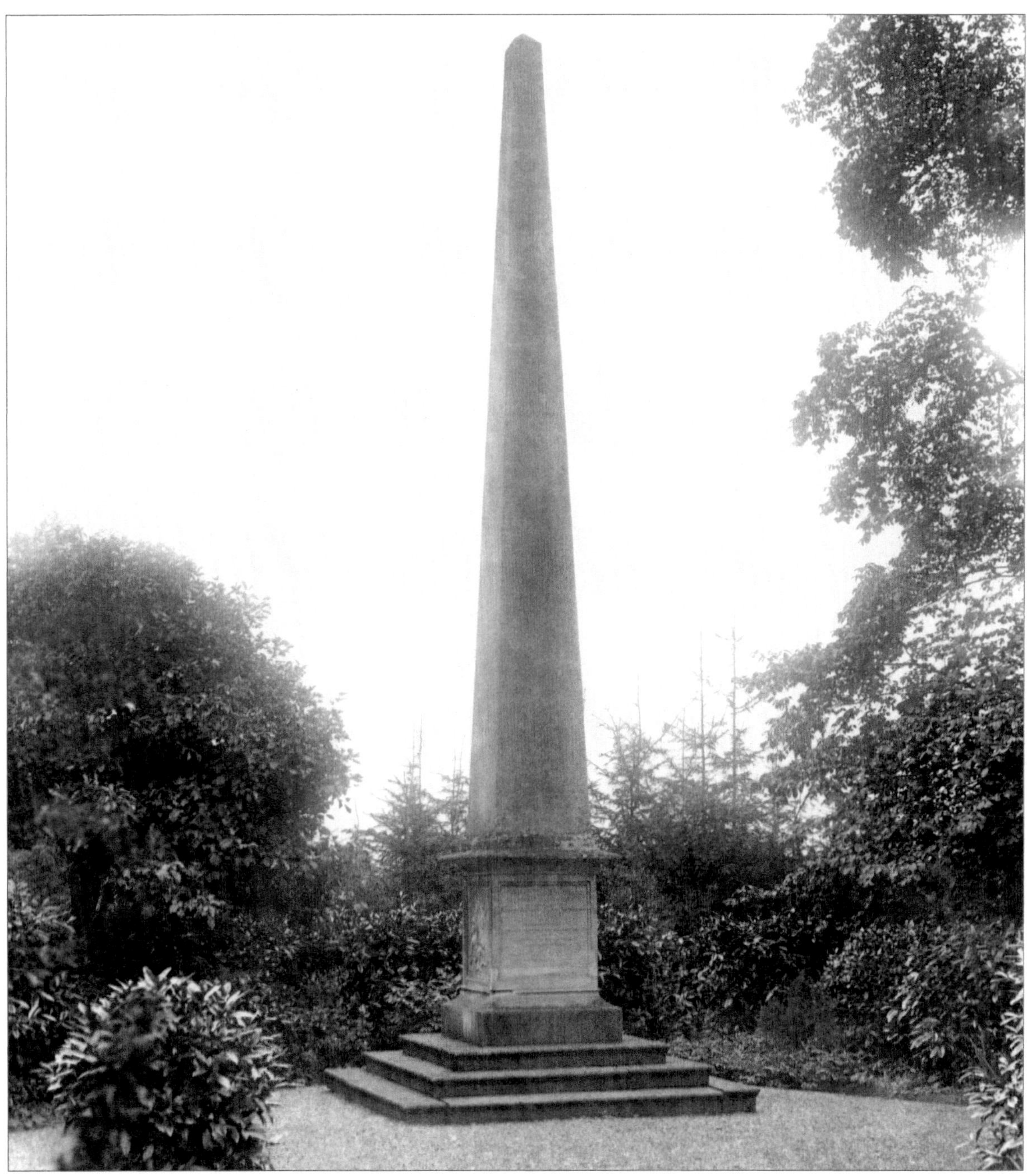

ABBEY MANOR, *The Obelisk 1899* 44119

Abbey Manor was built 1817-18 in extensive parkland to which concessionary access is available to those wishing to visit this obelisk, built in the 1840s to commemorate the Battle of Evesham, which was fought nearby. Elsewhere in the park stands the far more impressive Leicester Tower, a memorial to Simon de Montfort, Earl of Leicester, who died in the battle.

▼ **WOOD NORTON,** *The Hall, The Entrance Gates 1910* 62352a

In 1897, Wood Norton Hall was inherited by the Duc d'Orleans, a member of France's deposed royal family. In 1907, when his sister Louise married the Spanish prince Don Carlos of Bourbon-Siciles, Evesham hosted its one and only royal wedding. The grandson of Louise and Carlos is now King Juan Carlos of Spain. The Duc d'Orleans left Wood Norton in 1912 and the hall was bought by the BBC in 1939 for use as an emergency broadcasting centre in the Second World War. The BBC still has an engineering training centre on the estate, but the hall itself is now a hotel and conference centre.

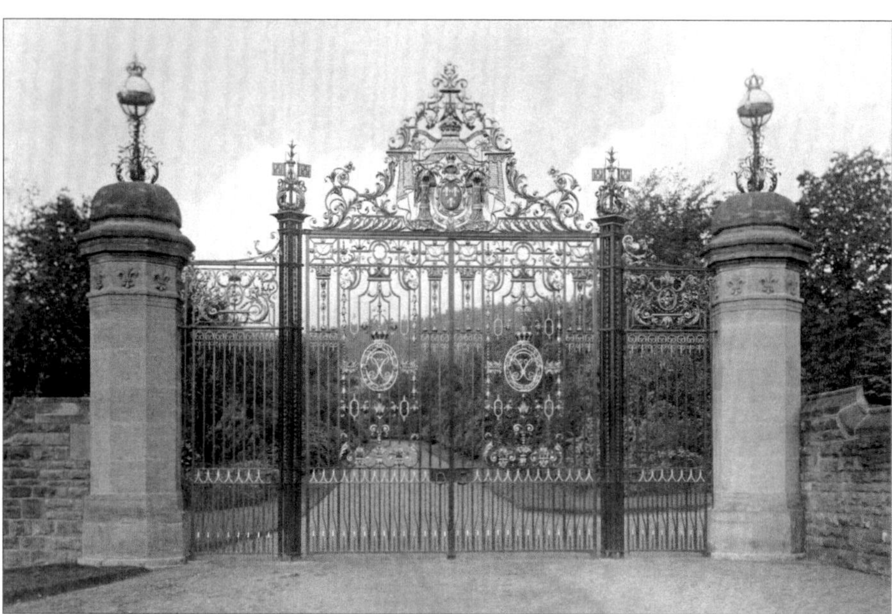

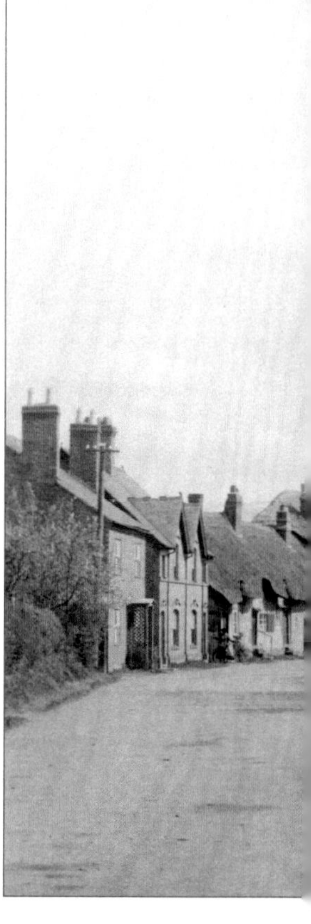

▶ **WYRE PIDDLE,** *The Village c1965* W312021

The medieval cross, rebuilt in 1844, marks the centre of this village on the north bank of the Avon between Evesham and Pershore. The building on the left, with distinctive chequered brickwork, no longer sells Henley Ices, or anything else. In fact, the village has no shop now, though it has not lost all its amenities. The Anchor Inn is still trading, and a frequent bus service operates to Pershore, Evesham and Worcester. The house on the right is greatly changed: its chequered brickwork is hidden beneath a coat of render, and its sash windows have been replaced by modern ones.

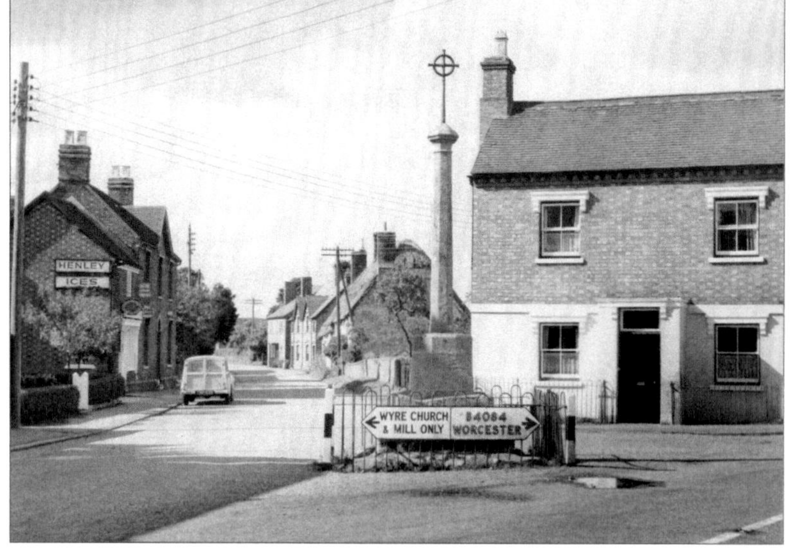

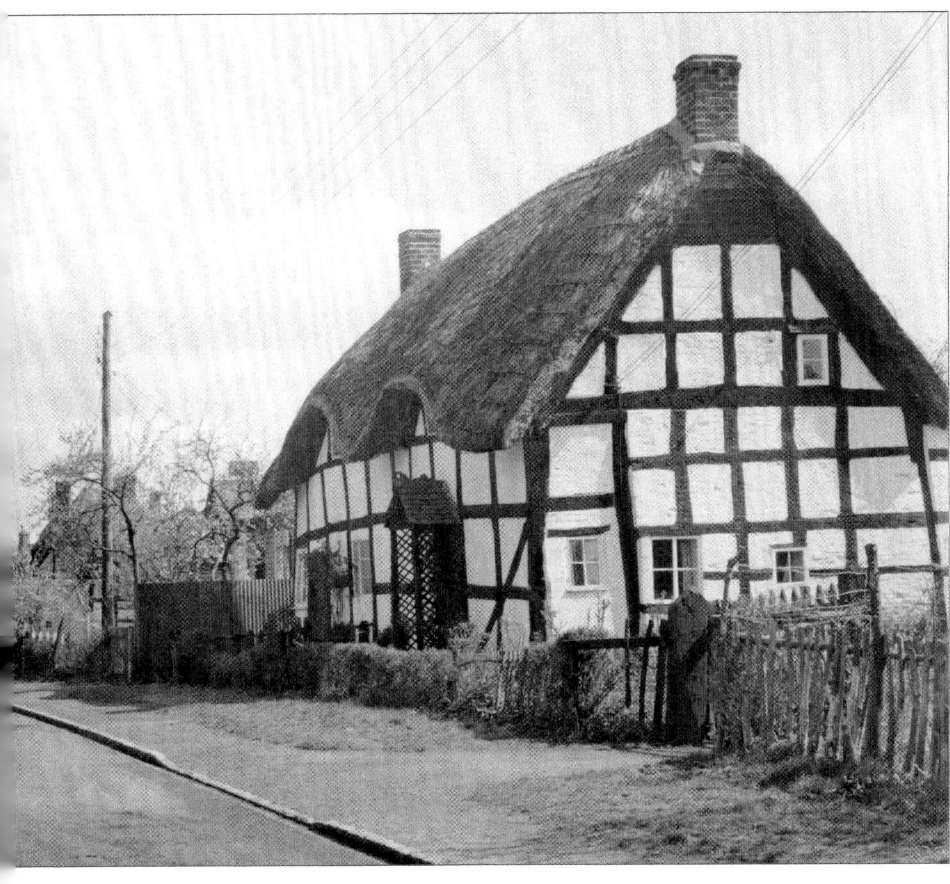

◄ WYRE PIDDLE
The Village
c1960 W312008

The timber-framed, thatched house survives, though much extended. The houses on the extreme left are still there too, but their charming thatched neighbours were demolished in the 1960s and replaced by modern houses. In fact, the village has been swamped by red-brick modernity - it nearly doubled in population almost overnight in the 1960s when a housing estate was built on a former farm.

► FLADBURY
The Church
1902 47320

It is likely that there was a Saxon church on this site, but no trace remains of it. Parts of the present building date from the 12th century, but a major rebuilding took place in 1340, with further restorations in 1865 and 1871 by local architect Frederick Preedy. It is commendable that part of the churchyard is managed as a conservation area, with wild flowers and long grass.

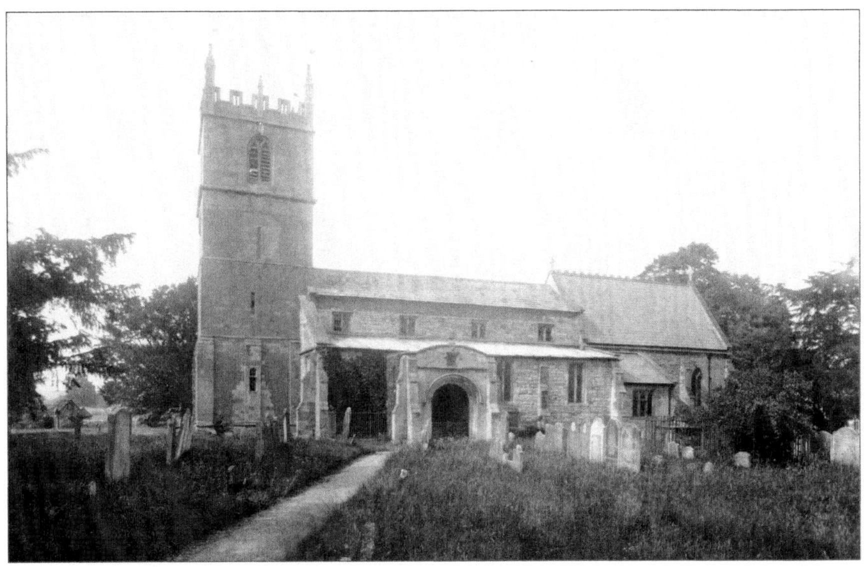

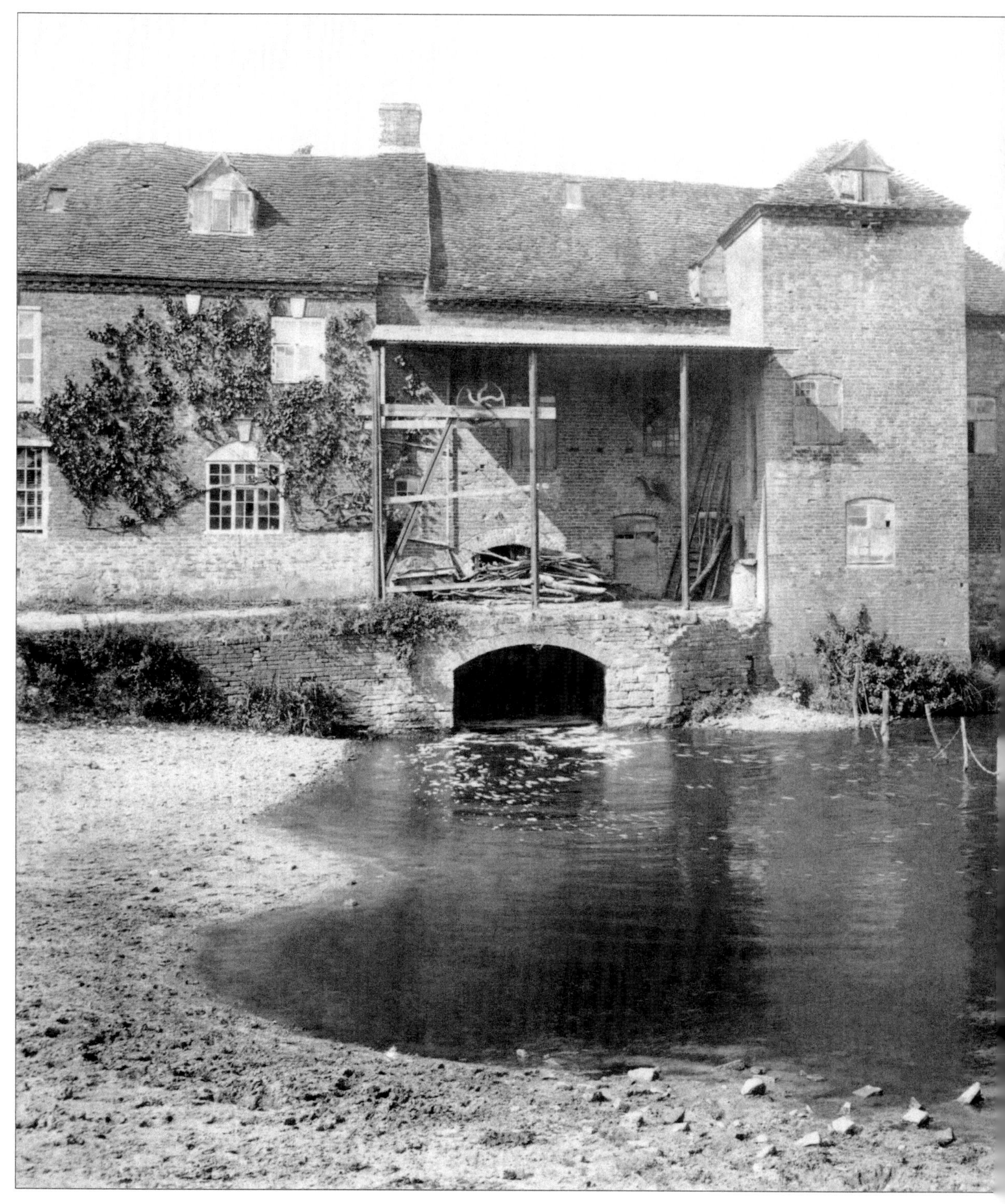

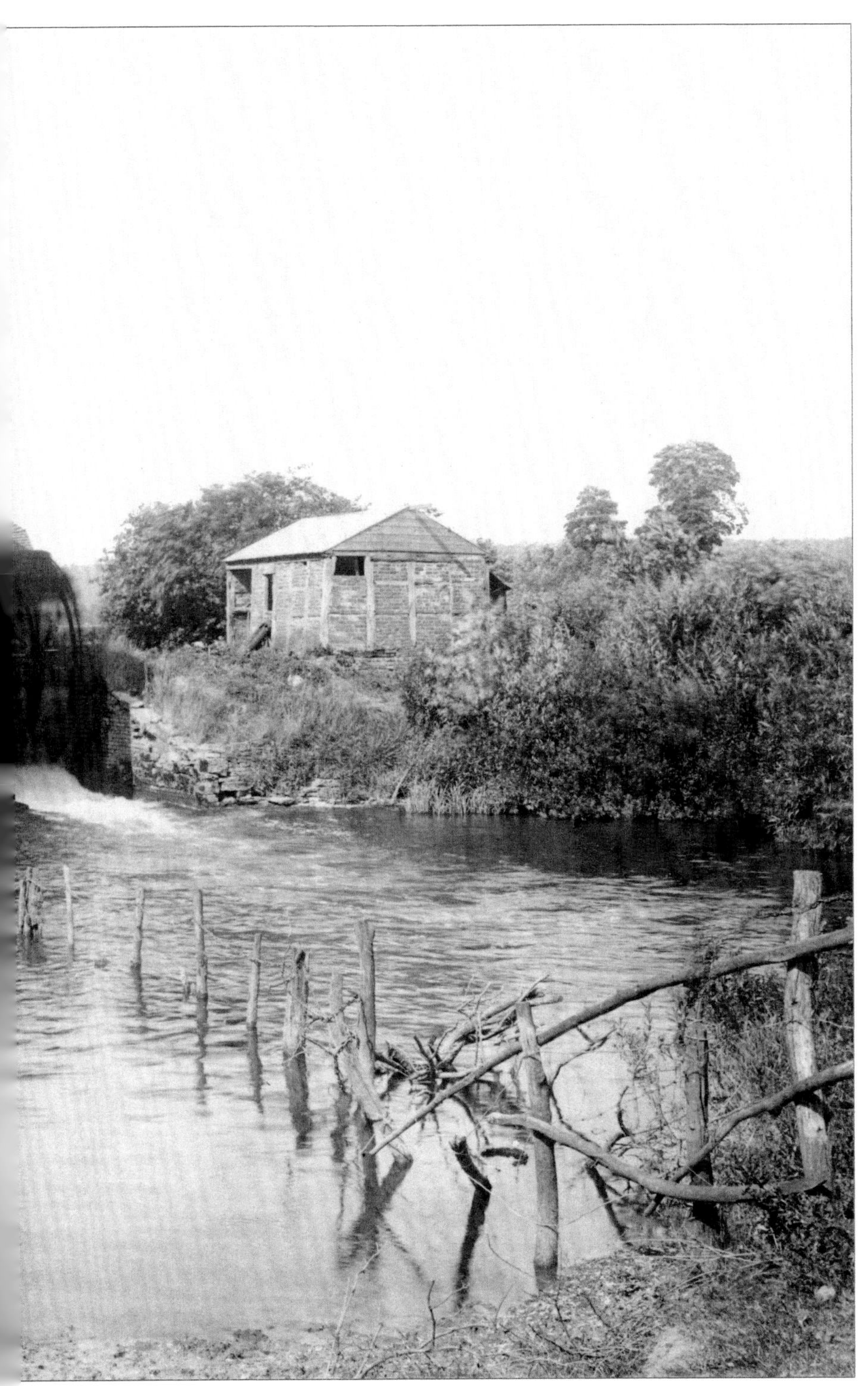

FLADBURY
The Mill 1899 44121

The oldest parts of Fladbury Mill probably date from the 16th century, and it remained in use until 1930. There was an earlier mill on the site, however, for one is recorded in the Domesday Book (1086). Corn was ground here for centuries, and the mill was also used for cider production at one time. In the late 19th century the Fladbury Electric Lighting & Power Company Ltd was formed. It used the mill to generate power, and in February 1900 Fladbury became one of the first villages in the country to have electric light.

FLADBURY
*The Lock and the Ferry
1902* 47319

There were two ferries at
Fladbury. One was a public
ferry which was hand-hauled
to the north end of the lock
island; the other was private
and used by the occupants
of Cropthorne Mill. It was
operated by a rope stretched
across the weir stream to the
mill and passing through
two brackets fixed to the flat-
bottomed boat.

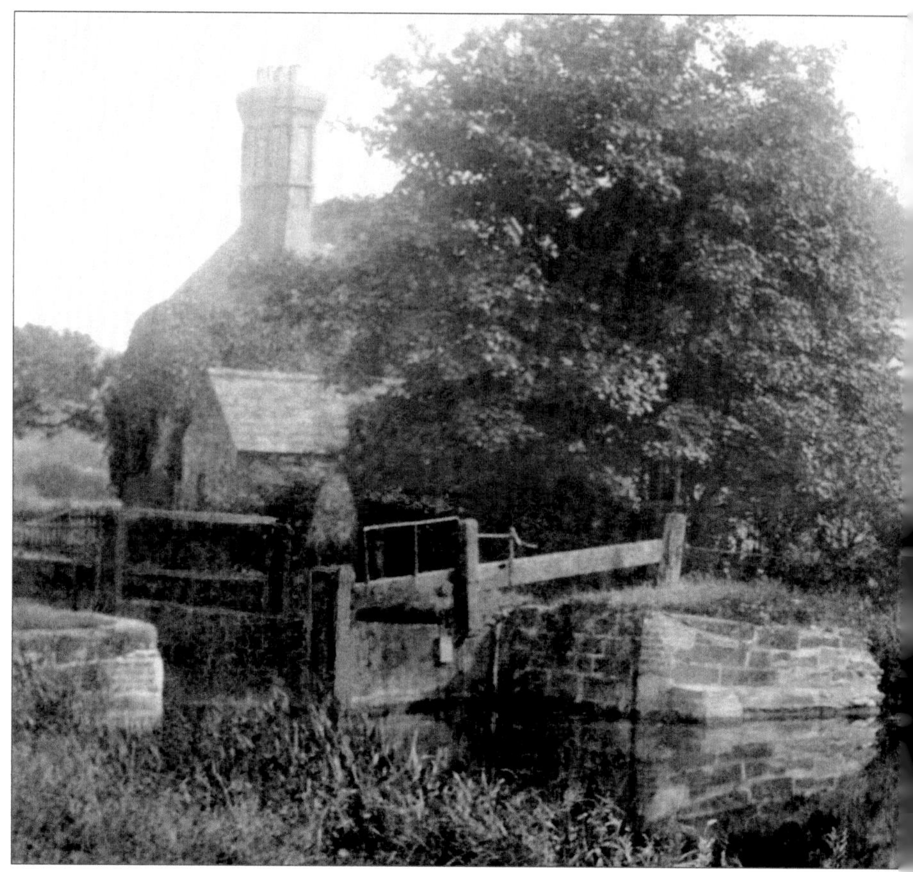

CROPTHORNE
The Mill 1910 62354

Despite its name, the mill stands by
Fladbury Lock, just across the river
from Fladbury, and some distance
from the village of Cropthorne. The
confusing situation is a result of
the parish boundary running along
the River Avon at this point, so that
technically the mill is in Cropthorne.
This photograph is taken from
Fladbury. From one or other of only
two places in the village where the
public had riverside access at that
time. One was Ferry Lane, a wide
grassy track leading to the water's
edge. The other a few yards away, was
a former coal wharf. Since summer
2006, access has also been made
available to Fladbury Mill meadow.

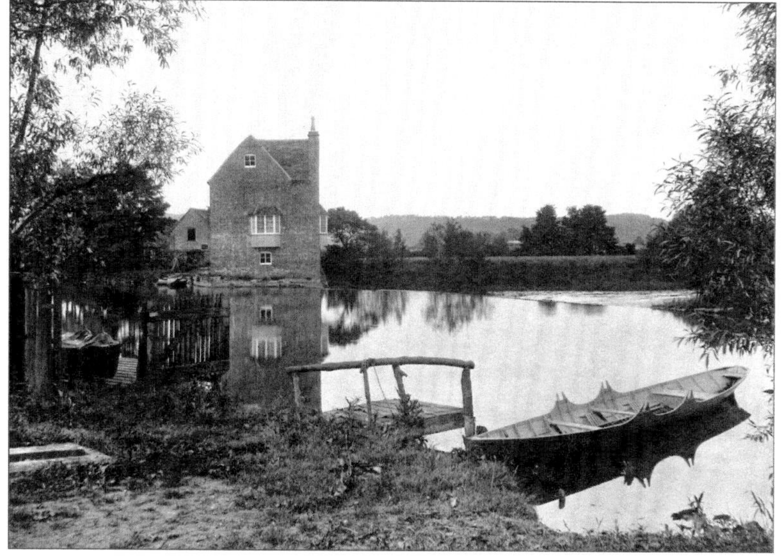

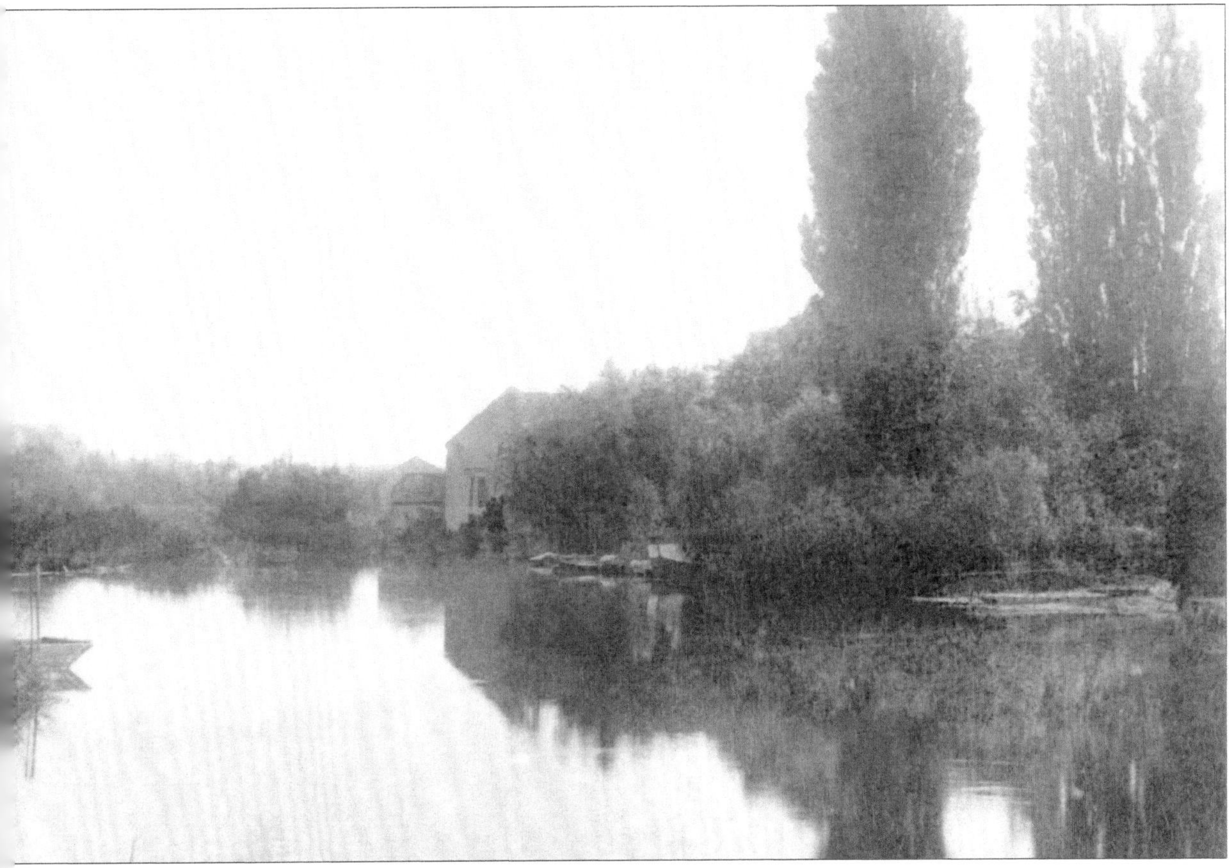

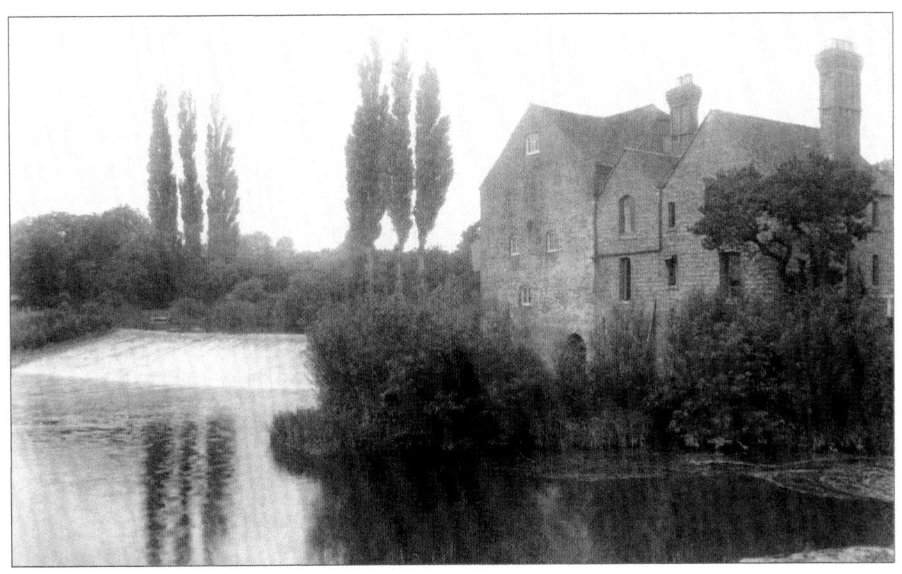

CROPTHORNE
The Mill 1899 44122

Taken from the Cropthorne side of the Avon, this photo reveals something of the powerful character of Cropthorne Mill. A succession of mills has stood on this site, but the present one was built c1700 and ceased working c1900. Its position, facing Fladbury Mill across a shared weir, is a reminder of the ubiquity and importance of mills in the economy of earlier times.

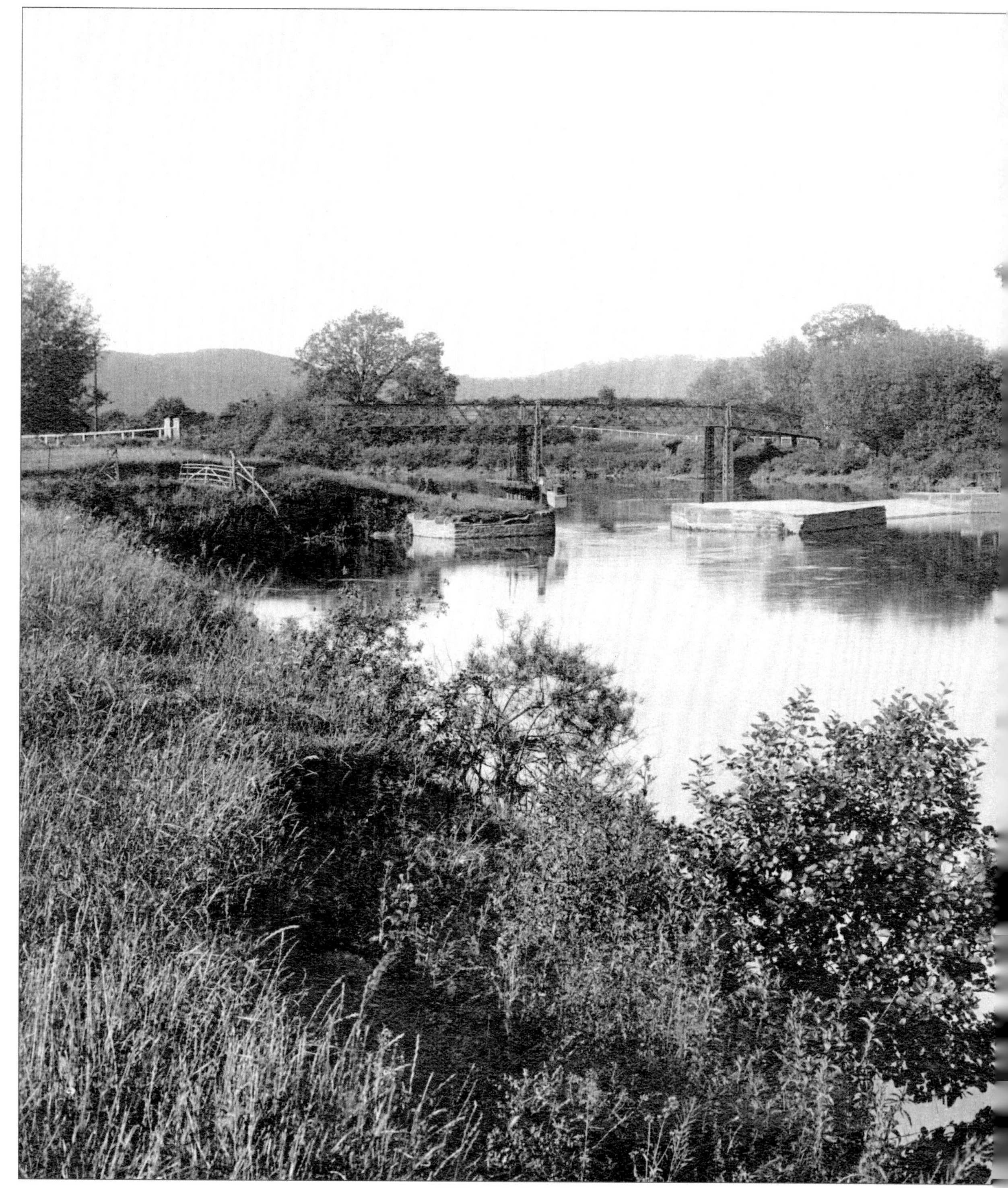

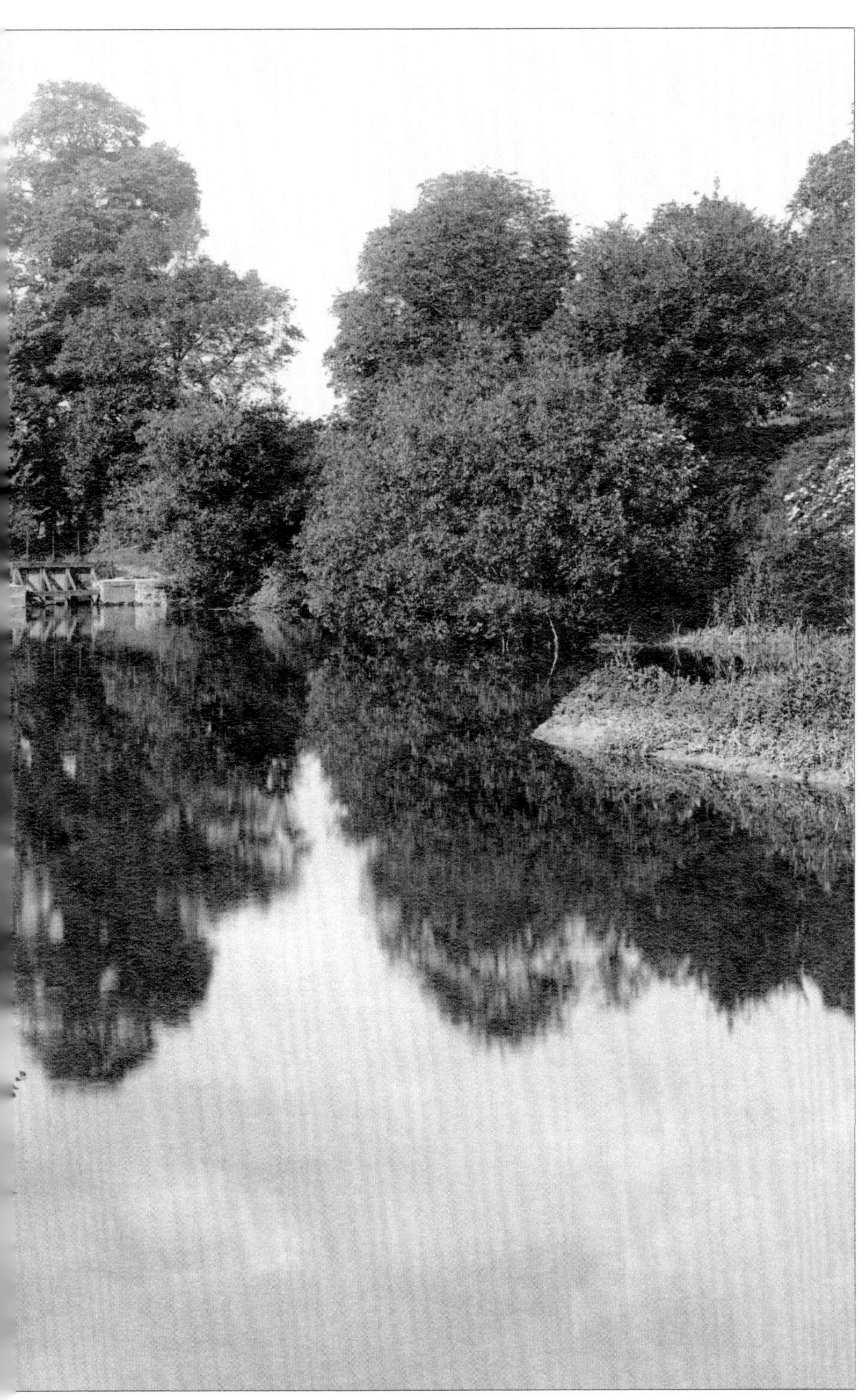

CROPTHORNE
The Weir and Jubilee Bridge 1910 62356

The rather ramshackle-looking Jubilee Bridge was erected in 1887 to commemorate Queen Victoria's Jubilee. It was rebuilt in concrete in 1933. There is no weir at this point today, but there was a ford here before the bridge was built and it was equipped with a watergate, consisting of gates and sluices set into a weir, which could be used to raise the water level when necessary. Such an arrangement was known locally as a wyre. Cropthorne watergate was demolished by the Lower Avon Navigation Trust in 1961 during the restoration of the navigation.

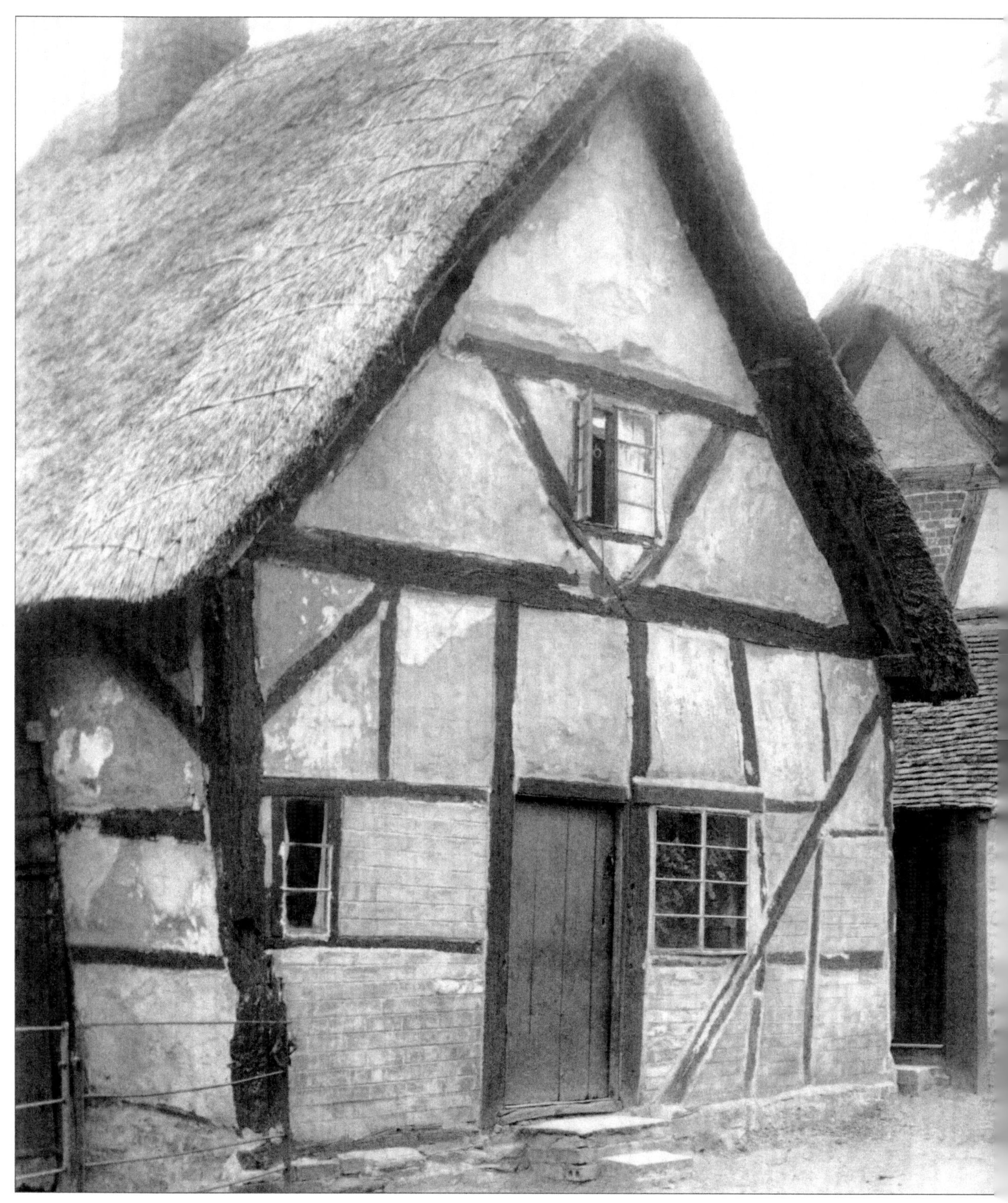

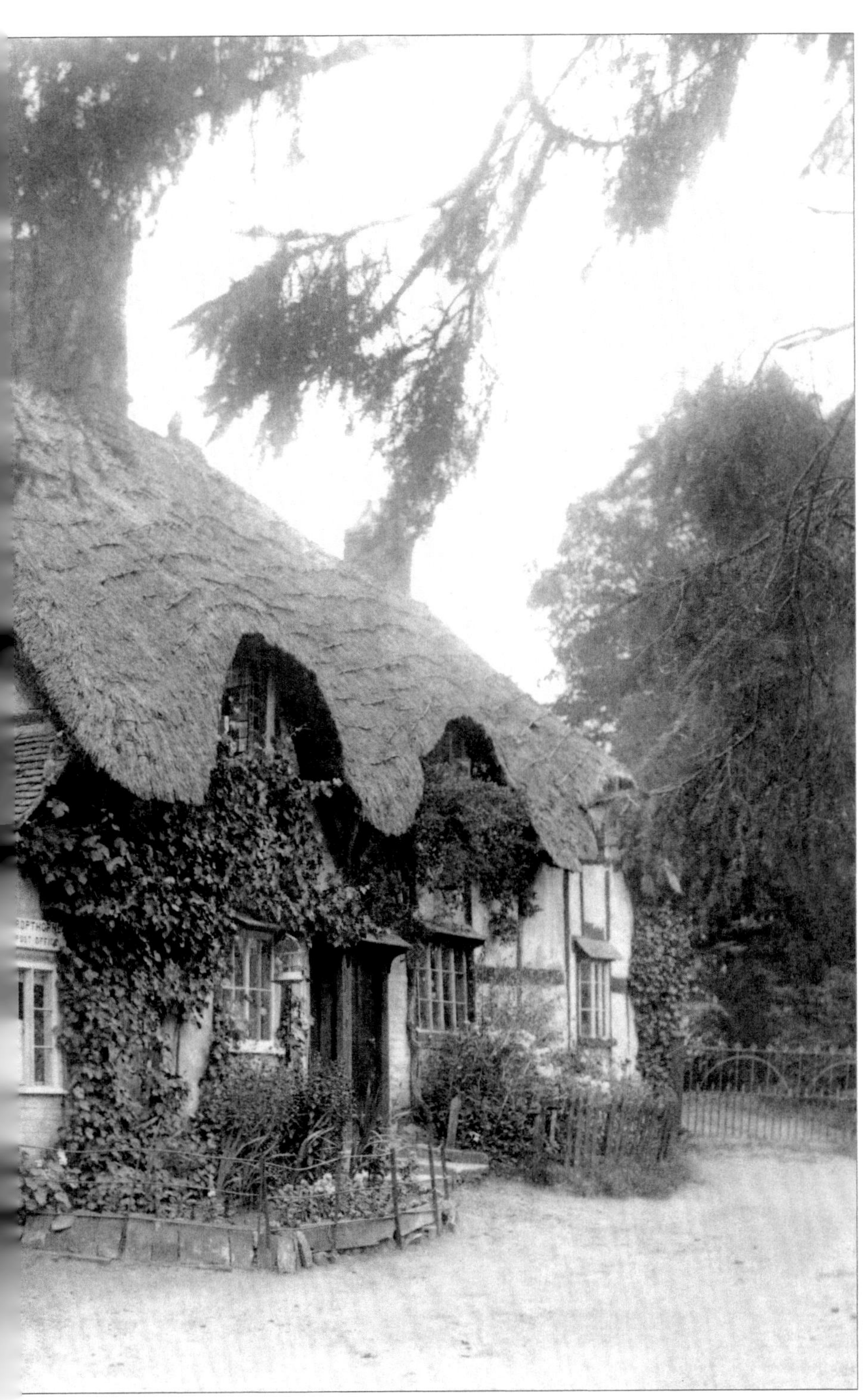

CROPTHORNE
The Post Office
1901 47322

The post office was originally in a large house now called The Pound House, but in the late 19th or early 20th century it moved to this location on Main Street. However, this is now The Old Post Office, as the post office has moved again. Unlike most old cottages, this pair has been fortunate - their restoration has been far more sensitive than the norm.

CROPTHORNE
The Church
1901 47323

St Michael's was founded before the Norman Conquest, but the earliest surviving work today is the base of the chancel arch, which dates from c1100. The church boasts a rare treasure: a cross-head which Pevsner declares 'the best piece of Anglo-Saxon art in the county'. It dates from cAD800, and is beautifully carved with foliage and mythical beasts.

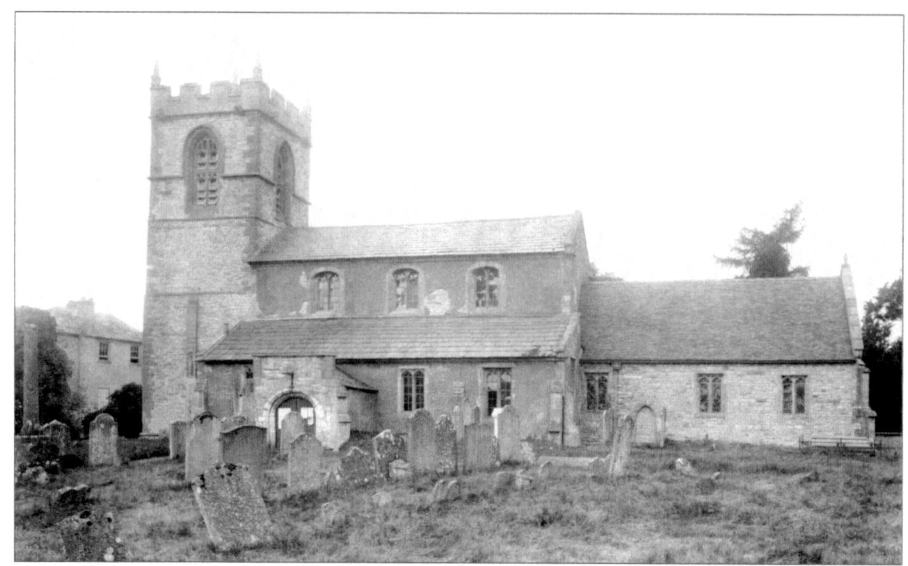

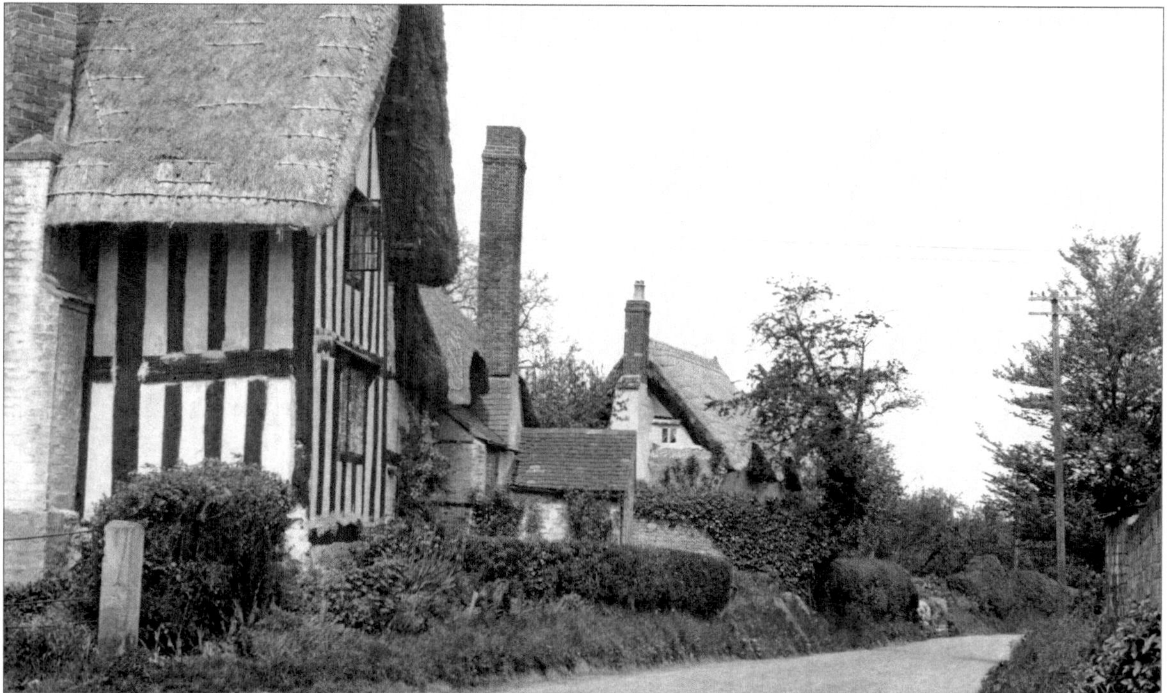

GREAT COMBERTON, *Cottages c1960* G331013

Great Comberton used to be surrounded by orchards of apples, pears and Pershore plums. Few survive today, but the surrounding countryside remains pleasant. A footpath called Quay Lane leads to the site of the quay on the Avon from which fruit was despatched to market. There are many timber-framed, thatched cottages in the village. This one is Whiteoaks, with Bank Cottage beyond it.

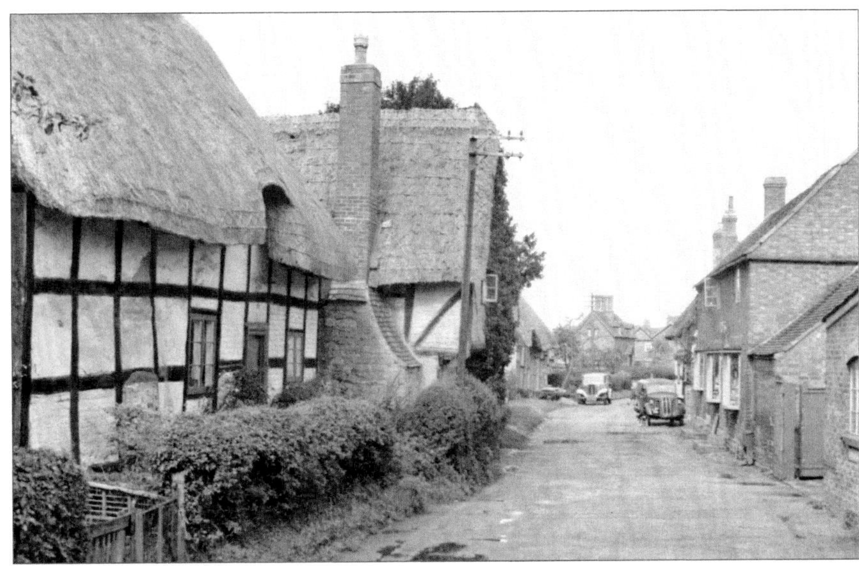

LITTLE COMBERTON
The Village
c1955 L216004

The timber-framed, jettied house second from left is Fern Dairy. Though it no longer functions as a dairy, it has been sensitively restored and re-thatched. The cottage directly opposite Fern Dairy goes by the name of Woodlouse House, but it was the village stores when this picture was taken.

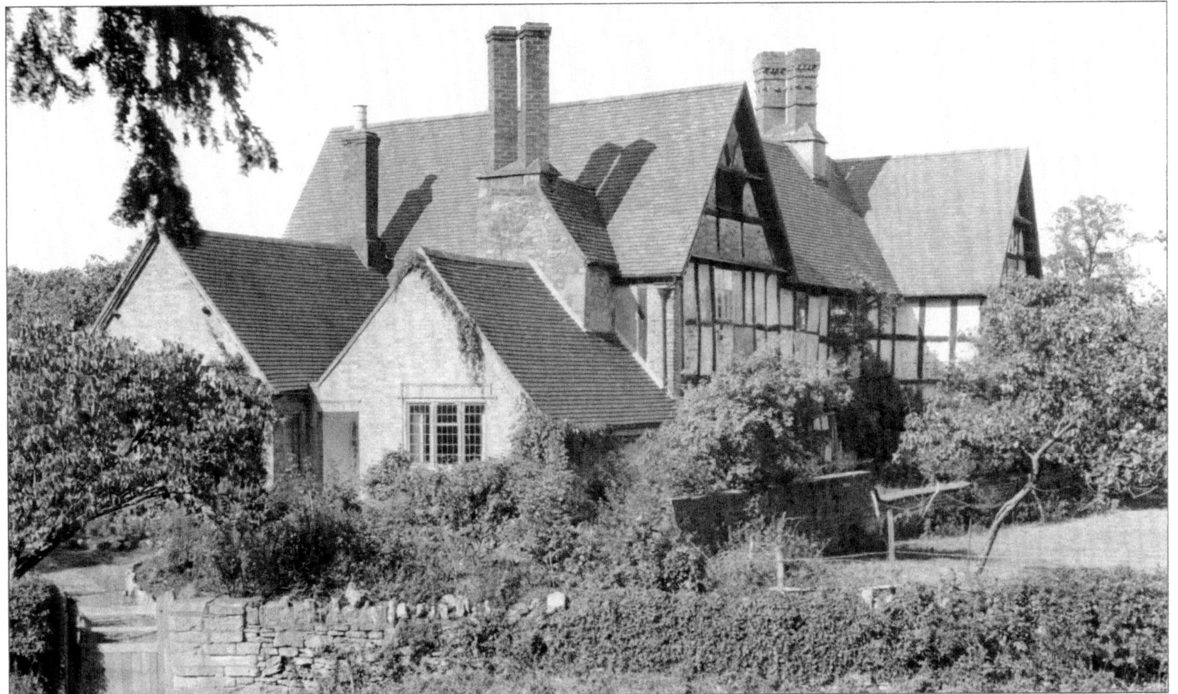

LITTLE COMBERTON, *The Old Manor House c1955* L216009

Taken from Manor Lane, this photograph reveals the side elevation of the Old Manor House, facing the church. The two gabled extensions are 20th-century rebuildings of much earlier extensions, one of which was brick, the other timber-framed. The house is probably of the 16th century; there is a local tradition that it was left by Henry VIII to his sixth wife, Catherine Parr.

▶ **LITTLE COMBERTON**
Bredon Hill
c1955 L216001

Bredon Hill is the largest of several Cotswold outliers, separated from the main escarpment in the Ice Age by meltwater torrents. It has a gentle dip slope to the south and a much steeper scarp slope to the north, overlooking the Vale of Evesham. A couple of seats in St Peter's Churchyard allow the visitor to sit and contemplate this view of the hill.

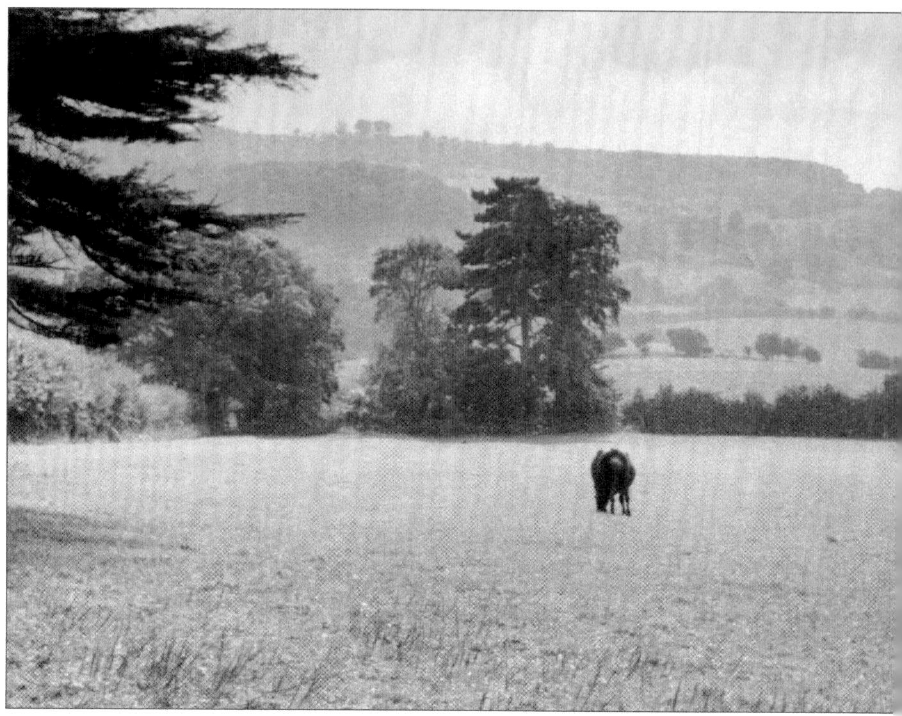

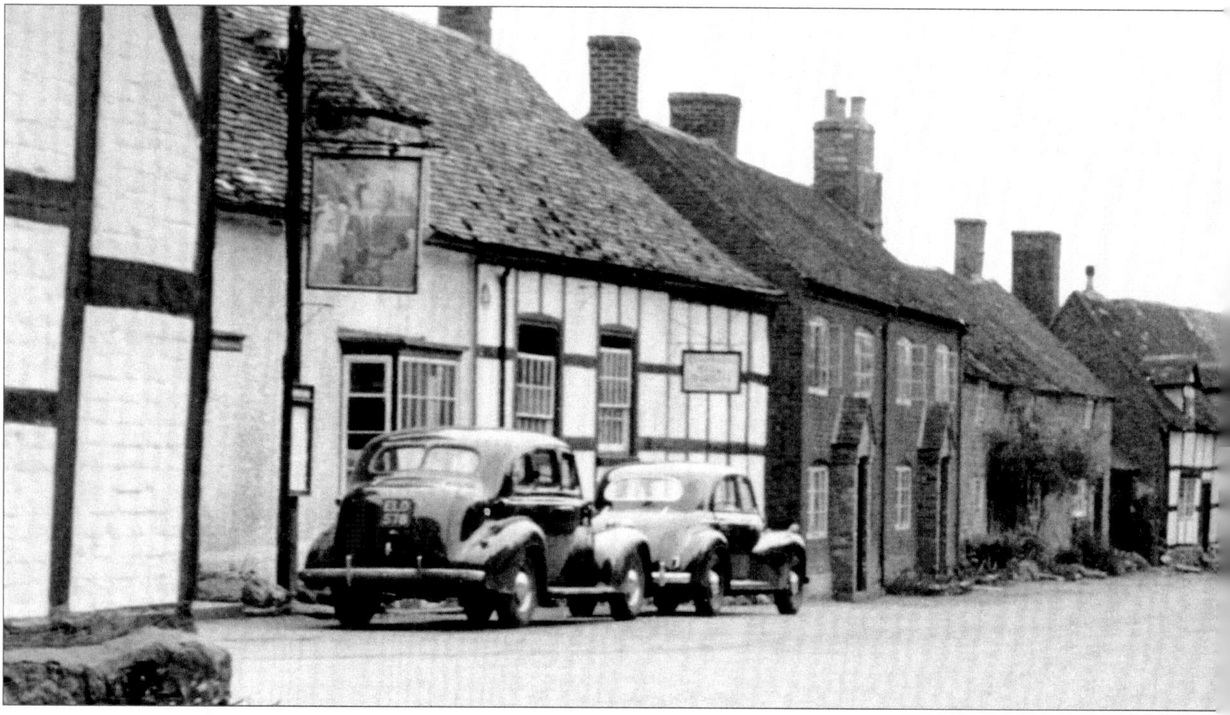

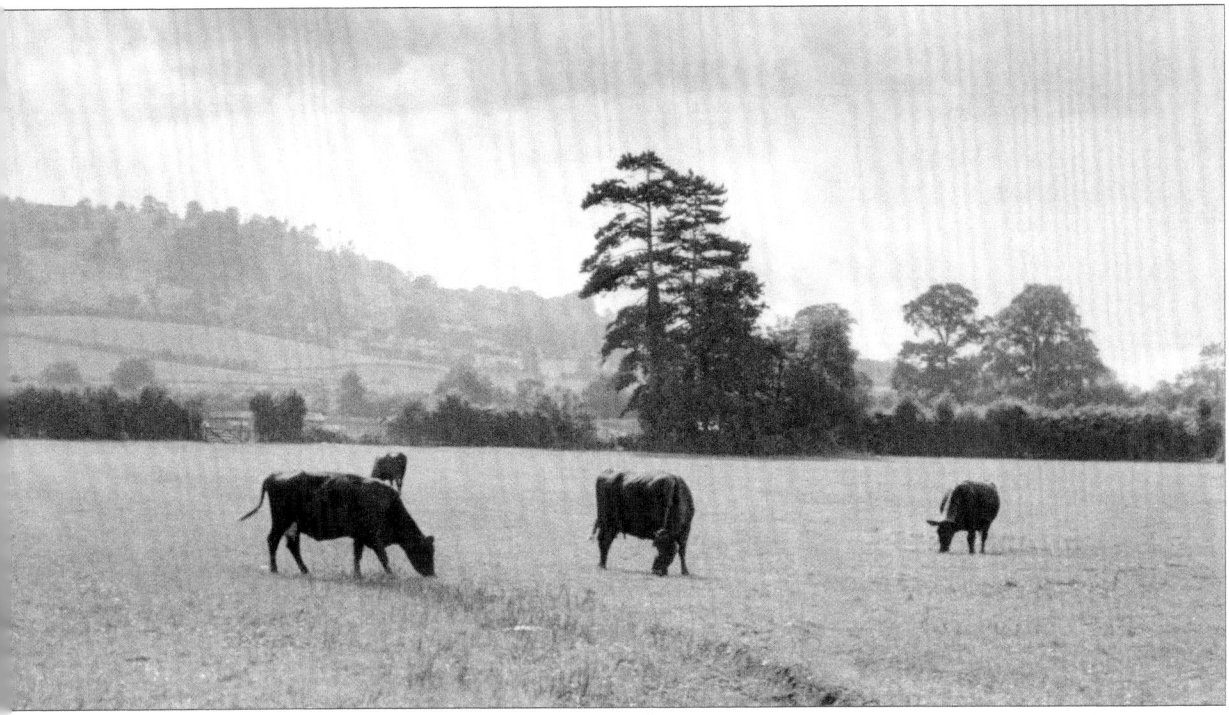

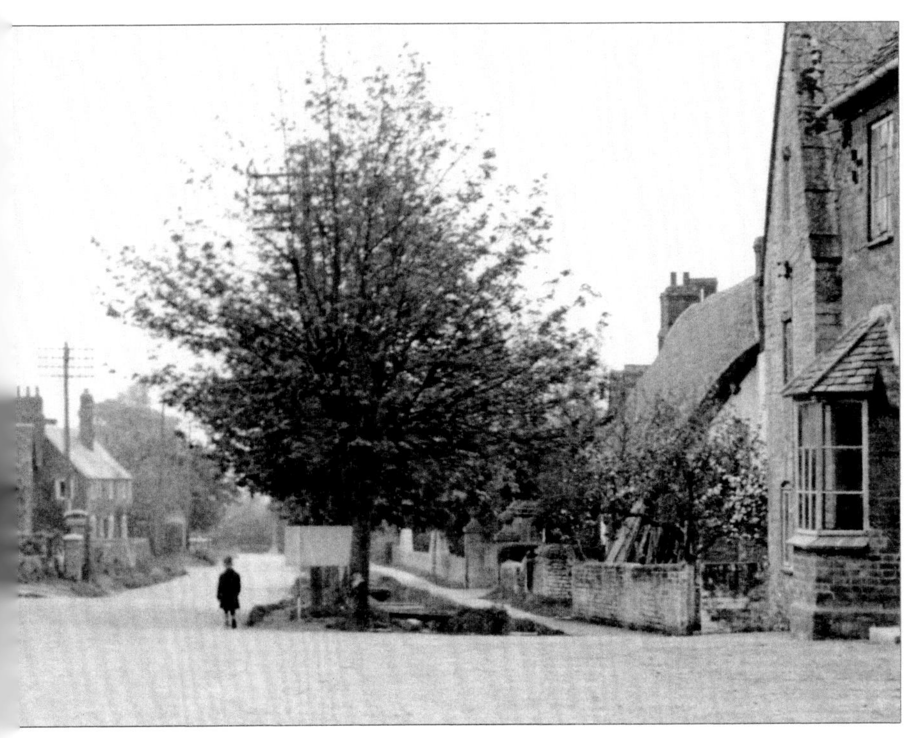

◄ **ELMLEY CASTLE**
The Village c1955
E108019

Lying south-east of the Combertons, below Bredon Hill, this village takes its name from an 11th-century castle, long since fallen into ruin. This is the main street, which remains largely unchanged. The pub behind the cars was formerly the Queen's Head but is now known as the Queen Elizabeth, and its colourful sign records the visit to Elmley Castle of Elizabeth I in 1575.

UPSTREAM FROM EVESHAM

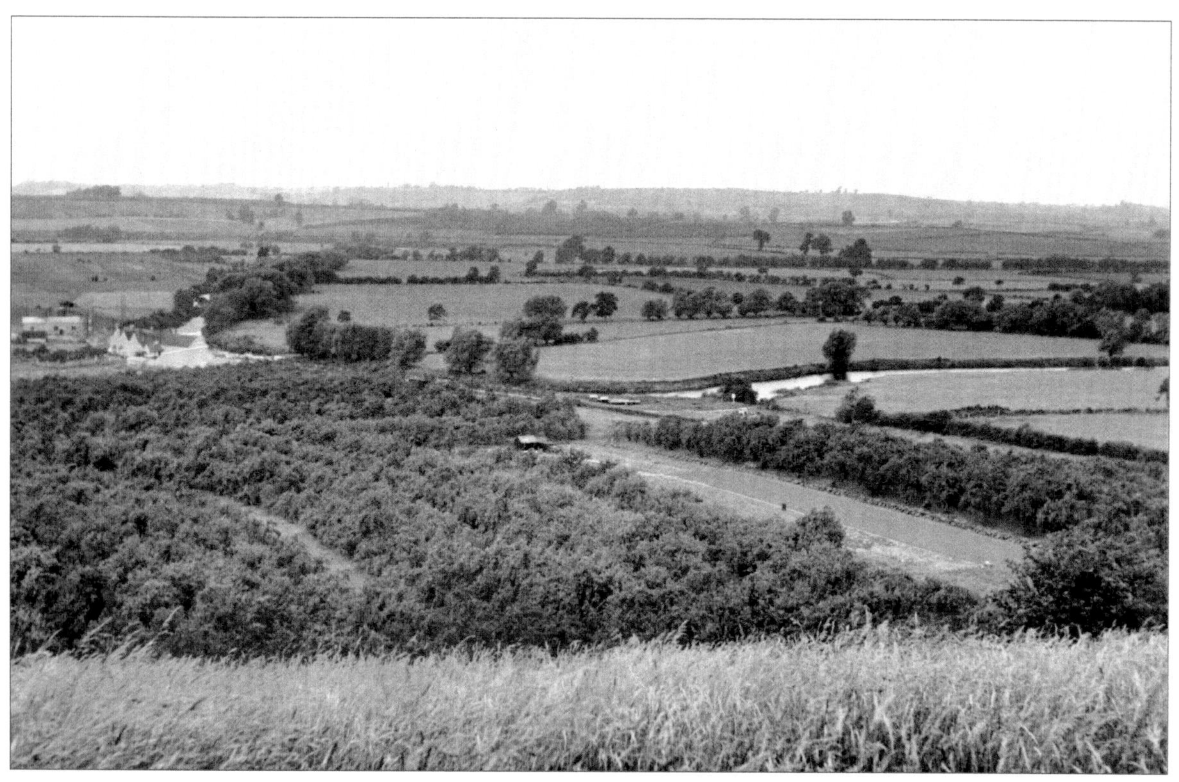

SOUTH LITTLETON, *General View*
c1960 S386005

This view of the vale is taken from somewhere on Cleeve Hill, to the north of South Littleton. The River Avon can be seen curving through the picture, and the prominent gabled building on the left is the Fish and Anchor, an old inn which stands beside a weir. Surveying the vale from a similar viewpoint today, one looks down on a caravan park and polytunnels, but no orchards.

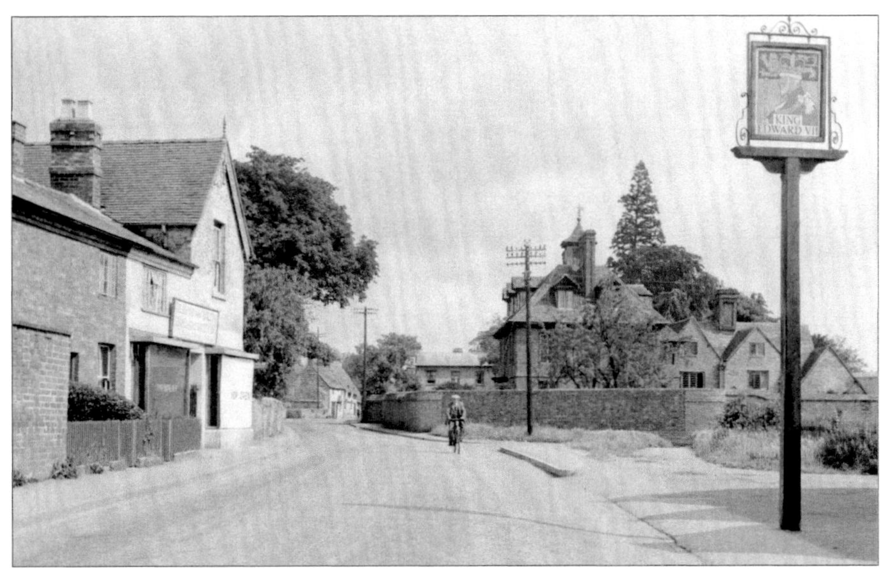

SOUTH LITTLETON
High Street
c1960 S386001

The unusual house on the right grew in stages over several centuries, probably from the 15th onwards, though the date on the cupola is 1721. The pub indicated by the free-standing sign has closed, and the building is now a private home, King Edward House. The Co-op shop on the left has closed too, but a Spar shop is now trading further down the street.

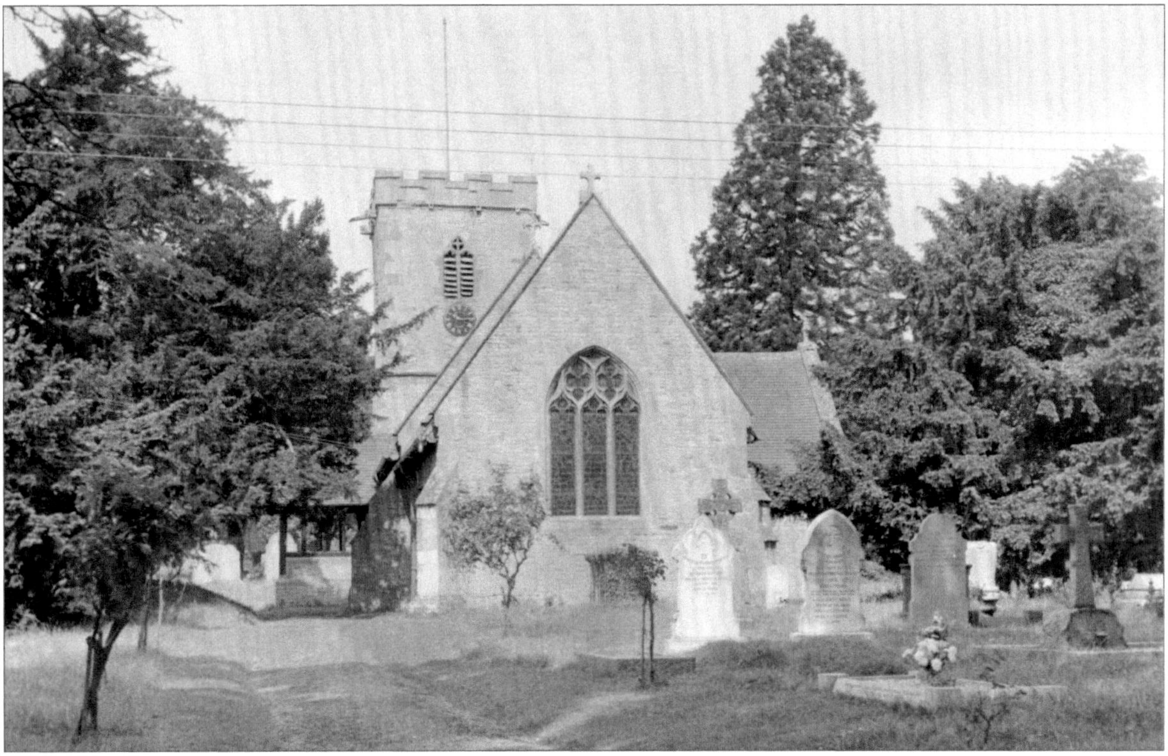

SOUTH LITTLETON, *The Church c1960* S386002

St Michael's is set back from Main Street, opposite the house featured in S386001, above. It combines Norman, 13th-century, 15th-century and Victorian work. A medieval preaching cross stands behind the yew tree on the left.

▼ MIDDLE LITTLETON, *The Church c1960* M406008

Middle Littleton almost merges with North Littleton, so St Nicholas's Church serves both. It is partly of the Early English period, but the Perpendicular south chapel was added by Thomas Smith, who died in 1532. The overall appearance of the church, however, is Victorian - it was restored by Frederick Preedy in 1871. There are some lovely, lichen-covered 18th-century headstones in the churchyard.

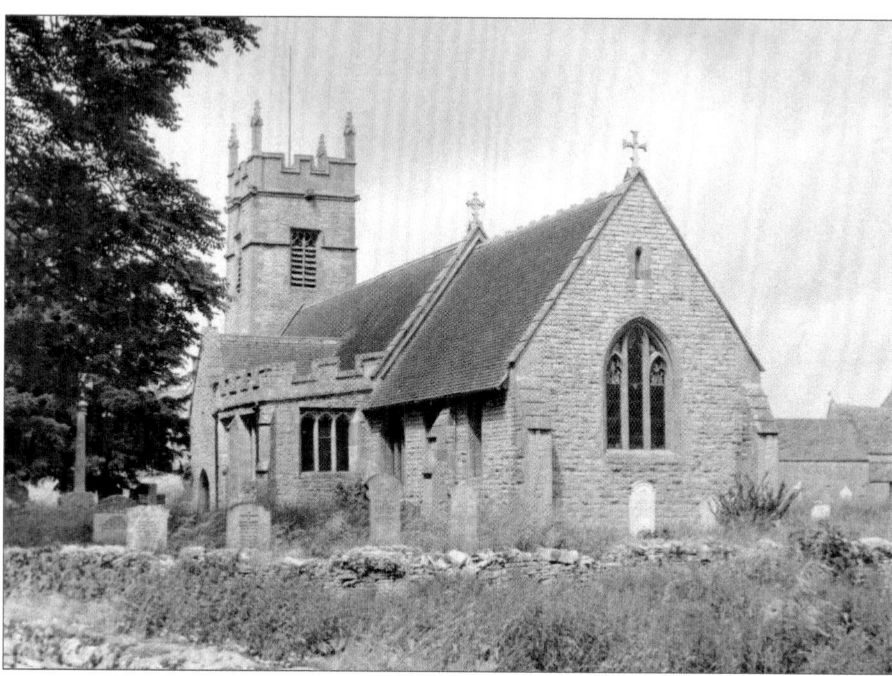

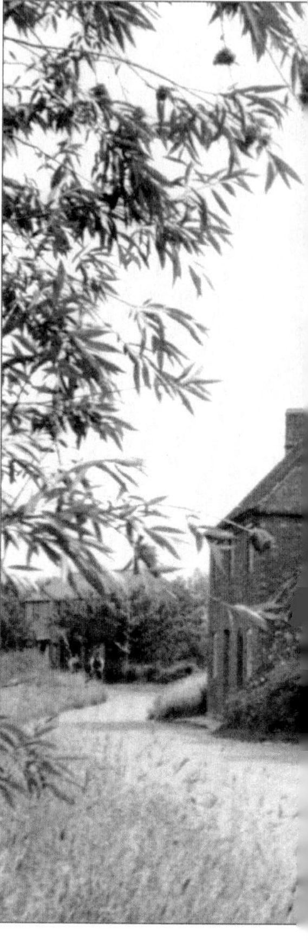

► MIDDLE LITTLETON
The Old Tithe Barn
c1960 M406010

This magnificent tithe barn was built for Evesham Abbey, though it is not certain exactly when. Documentary sources give us 1376, but carbon dating suggests a date of c1260. This is quite possible, because many monastic chronicles were written long after the events described, so discrepancies do occur. The barn is notable for its massive timber roof structure, which includes pairs of cruck beams, also indicative of an earlier date. In 1975 the barn was given to the National Trust, though it is still part of a working farm.

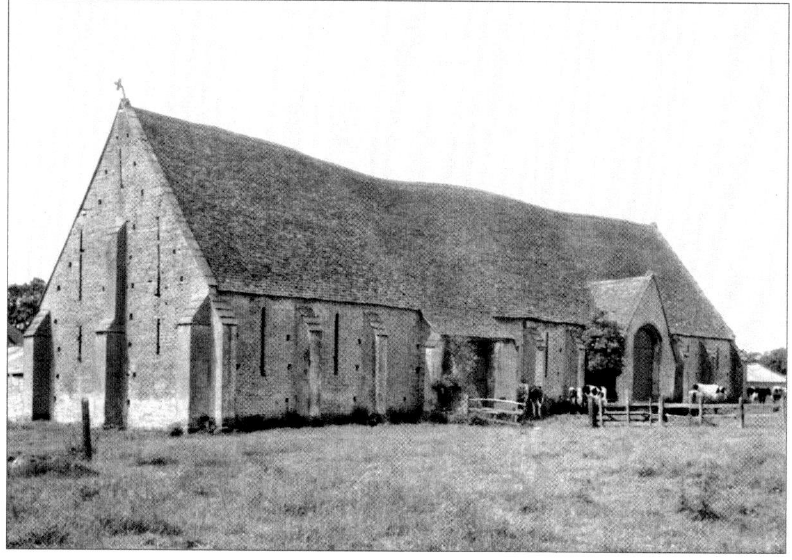

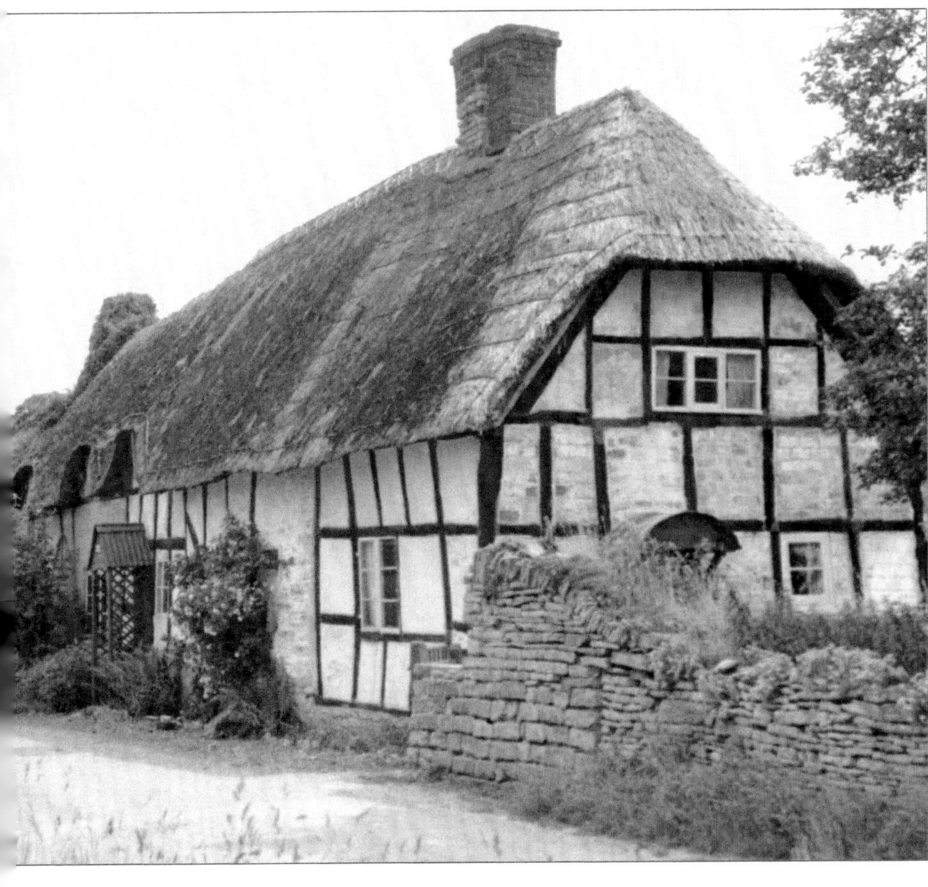

◄ NORTH LITTLETON
The Village
c1960 N220012

Approaching North Littleton on foot on a bridleway from Cleeve Prior, one comes first to these cottages at the northern end of a street called West Side. They bear little resemblance to this photograph, however, having acquired modern roof tiles, dormer windows and 1970s window frames.

► NORTH LITTLETON
The Village
c1960 N220013

Further south along West Side from N220012 (above), these cottages are easily recognisable. The gabled house in the middle, formerly the post office, is being sensitively restored at the time of writing. In the distance, beyond the van, there are modern houses now. In fact, the former hamlet is dominated by 20th-century houses which have no connection with the local vernacular.

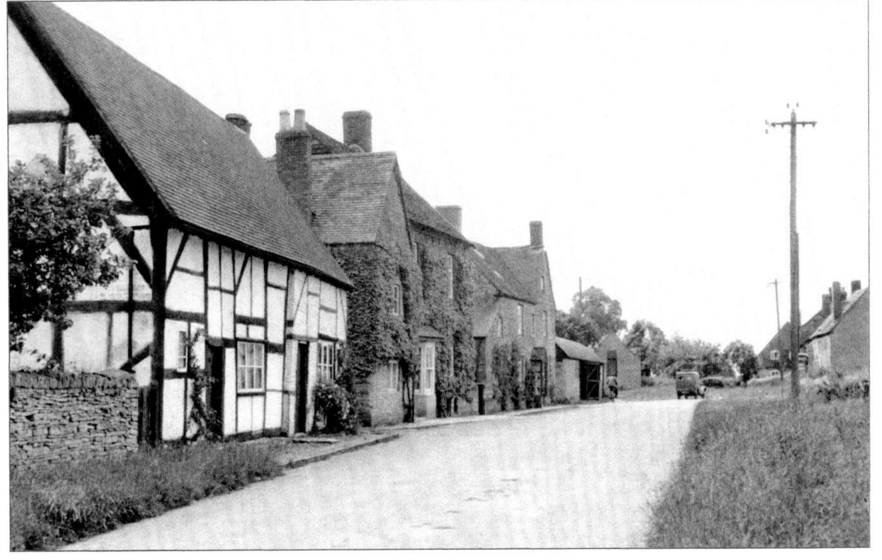

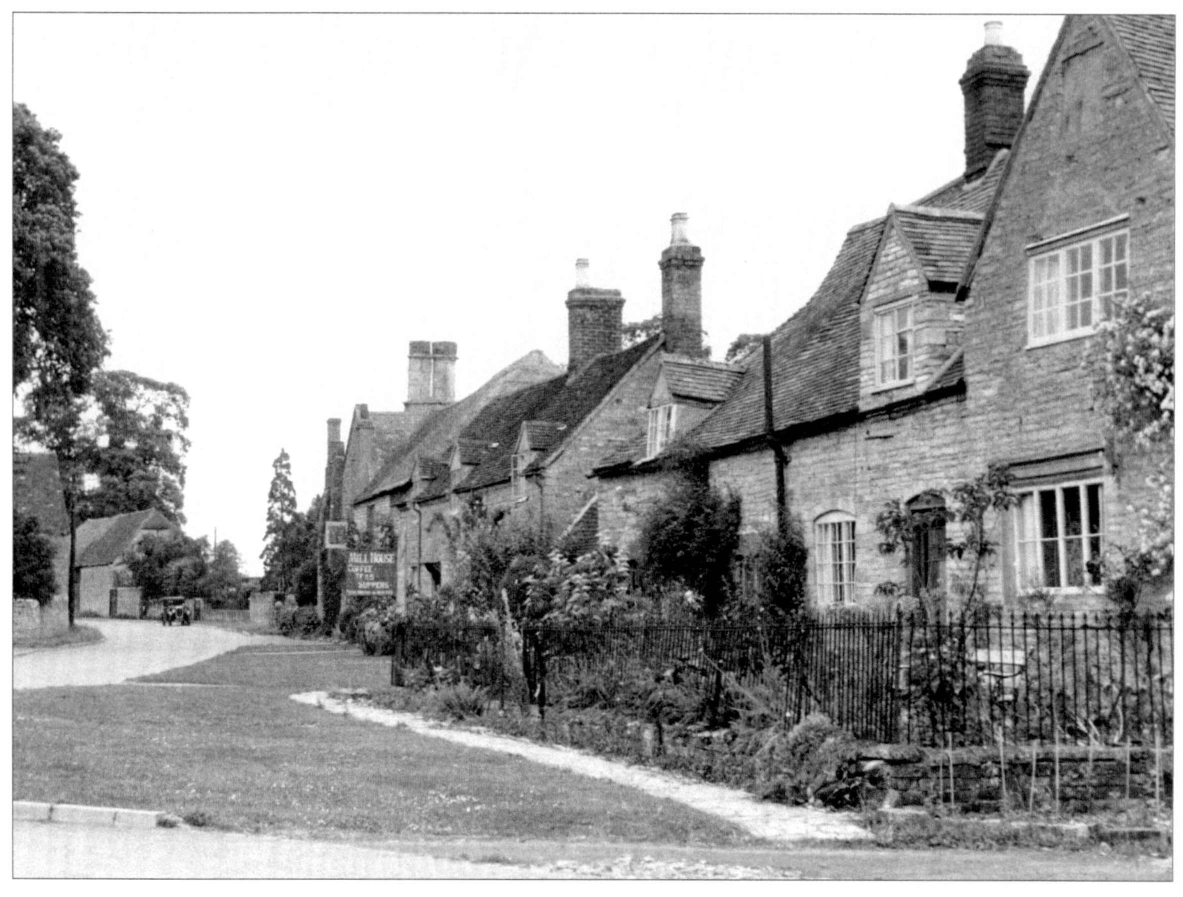

CLEEVE PRIOR
The Village c1955 C329004

North of the Littletons, high above the Avon, this is a village of
considerable character. The sign of the Kings Arms can just be
glimpsed at the left-hand end of this row of buildings. Still trading
today, it is said to have been serving ale since at least 1485. Next
to it in 1955 was Mill House, its sign advertising coffee, teas and
suppers. Today, it is The Old Cider Mill, a private house.

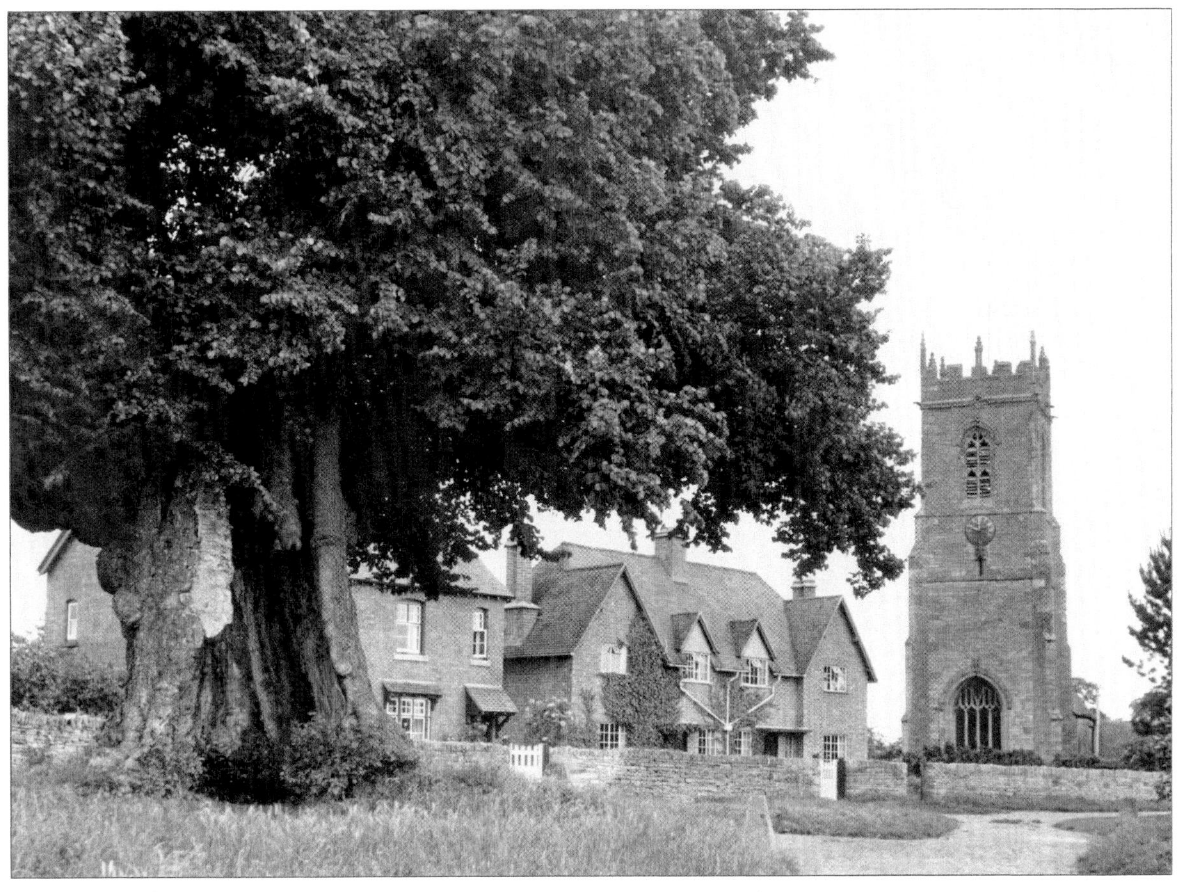

CLEEVE PRIOR
The Green and the Church c1955 C329005

St Andrew's Church was partly rebuilt in 1863 but remains a
lovely building with a commanding 14th-century tower. There is
a superb collection of carved 17th- and 18th-century headstones
in the churchyard. The most famous is that to Sara Charlett, who
died in 1693 at the age of 309 - or so it says on the stone. It is
assumed that the mason was having an off day.

▶ **CLEEVE PRIOR**
The Old Elm
1901 47333

This tree was believed
to be 300 years old
when it succumbed to
Dutch elm disease. An
oak has been planted
in its place. The
topiary peacock in
the cottage garden is
still maintained, and
is thought to be about
200 years old. Perhaps
it was inspired by the
fact that for many
centuries the vicar
was obliged to present
a peahen annually
to the church in
Worcester.

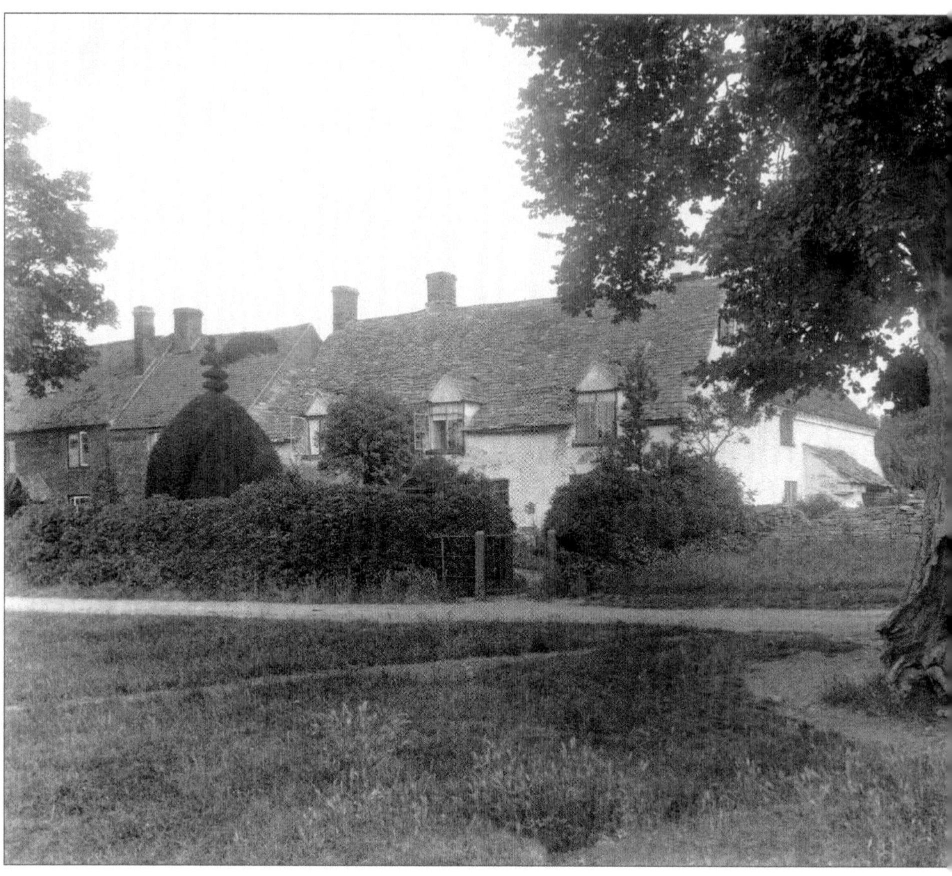

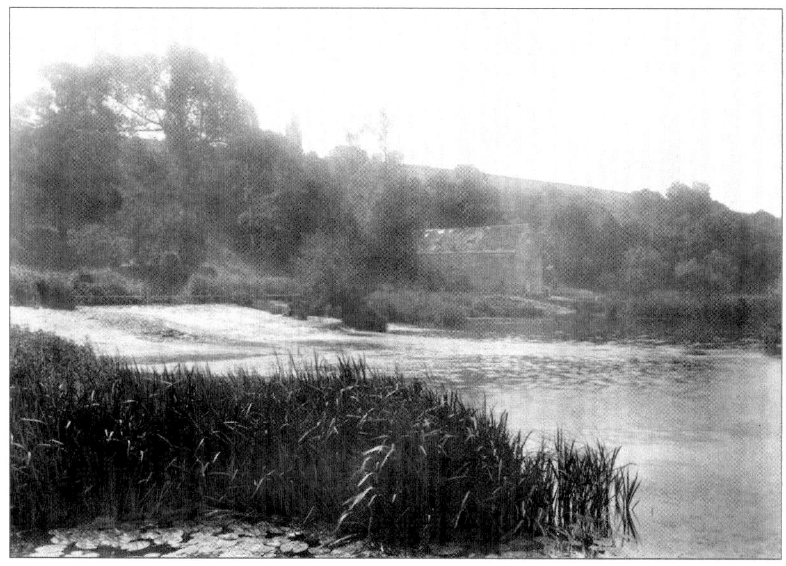

◀ **CLEEVE PRIOR,** *Cleeve Mill,*
The River Avon 1899 44123

This used to be a popular spot
with day-trippers, many of whom
arrived by steamer and enjoyed
cream teas at the mill, while others
would bring a picnic and hire a skiff
from the mill. It stood at the foot of
Cleeve Hill, below Cleeve Prior. Two
steep paths lead uphill, along with
a track called Mill Lane, formerly
used by wagons serving the mill.
Sad to say, the weir was breached in
1939, and the mill fell into disrepair
and was subsequently dismantled.
The weir was demolished and the
nearby ford dredged in 1970 during
the restoration of the Upper Avon
Navigation.

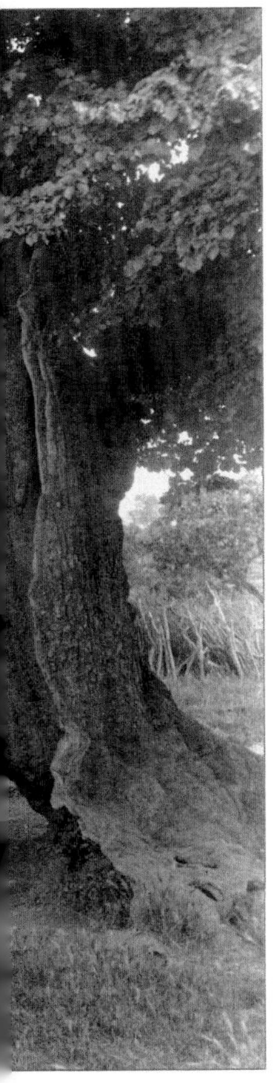

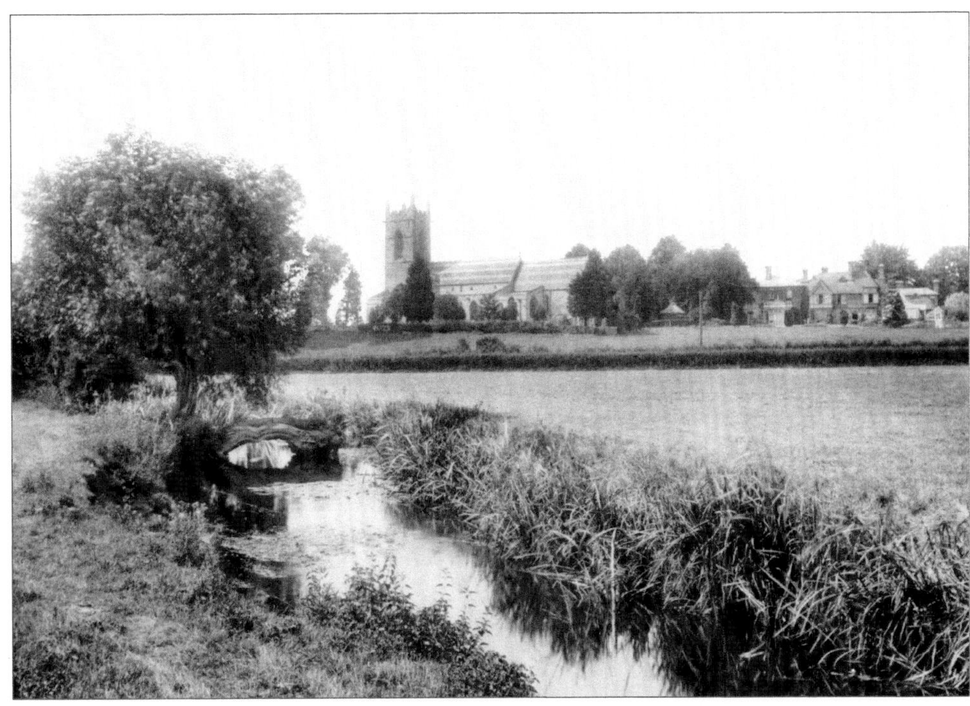

▲ **SALFORD PRIORS,** *The Church and the Vicarage 1901* 47330

One of only two Warwickshire villages in this book (the other is Abbot's Salford), this sits across the river from Cleeve Prior. It was originally known as Salteford Major and belonged to Evesham Abbey. In 1122 it was given to St Mary's Priory at Kenilworth and acquired its present name. St Matthew's Church was built in the 11th century.

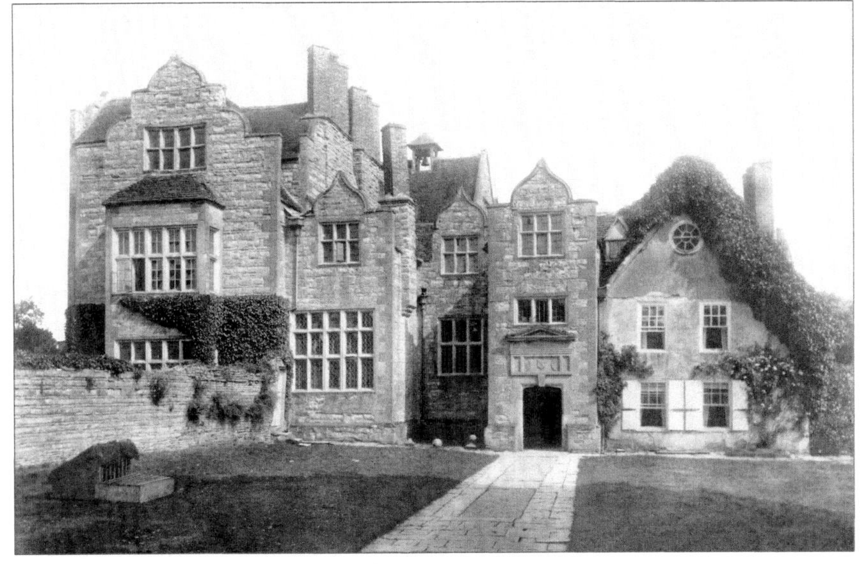

◄ **ABBOT'S SALFORD**
The Nunnery
1901 47331

Originally Salteford Minor, Abbot's Salford acquired its present name after an abbot of Evesham built himself a country house there c1470. Part of his house survives as the west wing of this building, which dates mostly from 1602-06. It served as a Benedictine nunnery from 1807 until 1838. It later fell into decay, but was restored c1970 to become the Salford Hall Hotel.

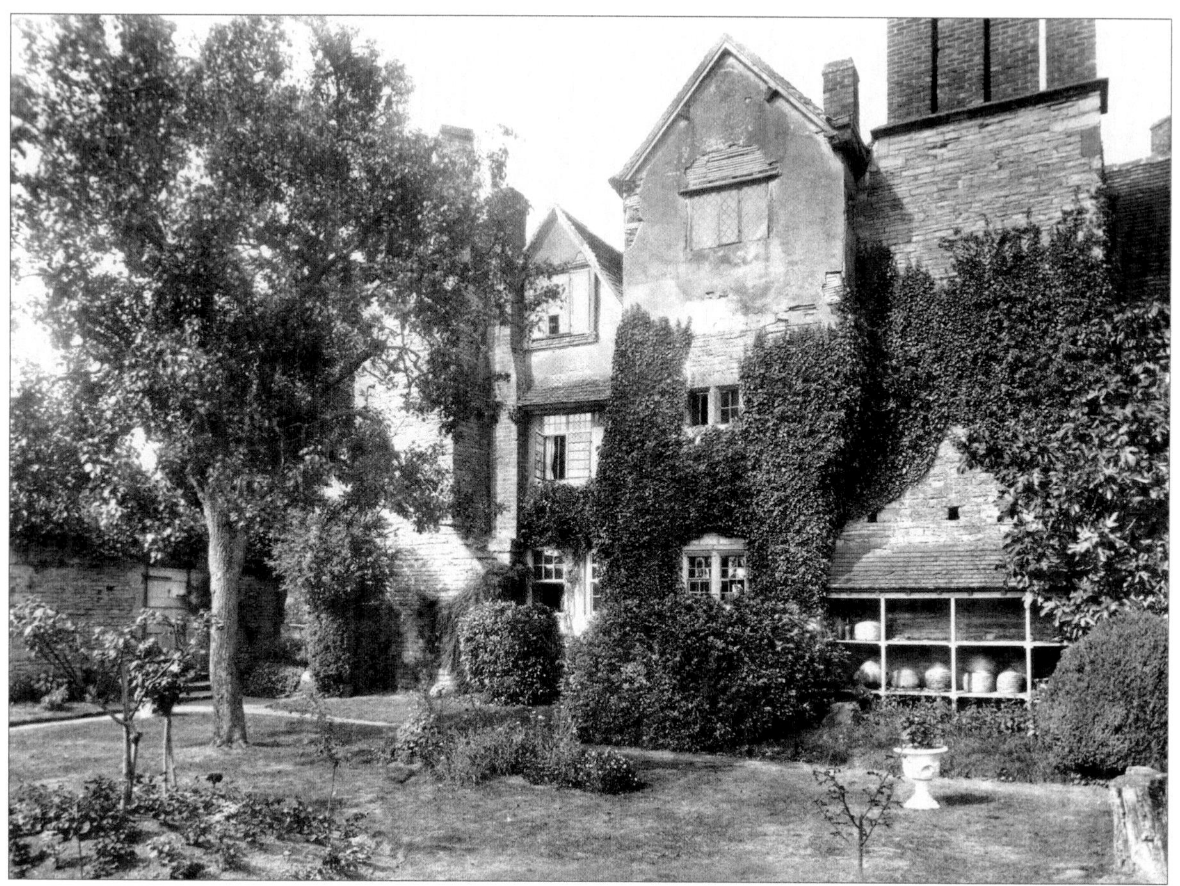

ABBOT'S SALFORD, *The Nunnery 1901* 47332

The dome-shaped baskets in the store attached to the wall
are bee skeps, in which honeybees were housed before the
invention of wooden hives. Skeps were usually made from straw,
but grass, reed or sedge might be used instead, depending on
local availability. There are two bee skeps similar to these in the
Almonry Heritage Centre in Evesham.

INDEX

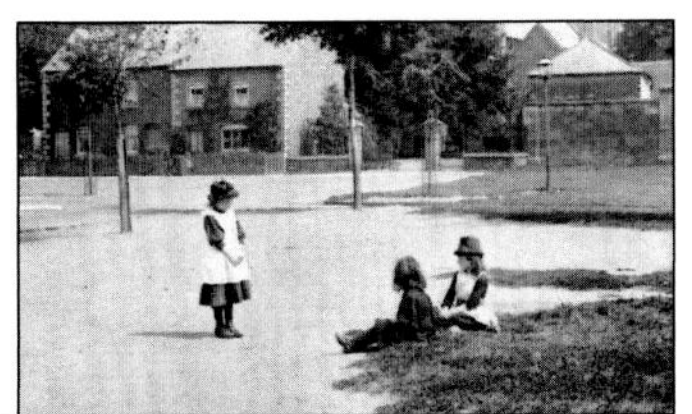

Abbey Manor 65

Abbot Reginald's Gateway 15, 24, 25

Abbot's Salford 87, 88

All Saints' Church 16, 17

The Almonry 21, 22, 23

The Bandstand 51

The Bell Tower 19, 48, 50, 52-53

Booth Hall 13, 28, 29, 30, 31

Bridge Street 40-41, 42, 43, 44-45, 46, 47

Chadbury Mill 64

Children's Boating Pool 50

Cleeve Prior 84, 85, 86-87

Cropthorne 70, 71, 72-73, 74-75, 76

The Crown Hotel 46

Daffodils 56-57

Elmley Castle 78-79

Fladbury 67, 68-69, 70-71

From Clark's Hill 64

Great Comberton 76

Hampton Church 60-61, 62

Hampton Ferry 63

High Street 32, 33, 34

Little Comberton 77, 78-79

Market Place 26, 27, 28, 29

Merstow Green 36-37

Middle Littleton 82

North Littleton 83

River and the Boathouse 52-53

River and the Bridge 10, 54-55, 56-57

River Avon 51, 52-53, 54-55

St Lawrence's Church 18

Salford Priors 87

South Littleton 80, 81

Vine Street 34-35

War Memorial and the Bell Tower 50

Woman and Child Near the Bell Tower 20

Wood Norton 66

Wyre Piddle 66-67

FRITH PRODUCTS & SERVICES

Francis Frith would doubtless be pleased to know that the pioneering publishing venture he started in 1860 still continues today. Over a hundred and forty years later, The Francis Frith Collection continues in the same innovative tradition and is now one of the foremost publishers of vintage photographs in the world. Some of the current activities include:

INTERIOR DECORATION

Today Frith's photographs can be seen framed and as giant wall murals in thousands of pubs, restaurants, hotels, banks, retail stores and other public buildings throughout the country. In every case they enhance the unique local atmosphere of the places they depict and provide reminders of gentler days in an increasingly busy and frenetic world.

PRODUCT PROMOTIONS

Frith products are used by many major companies to promote the sales of their own products or to reinforce their own history and heritage. Frith promotions have been used by Hovis bread, Courage beers, Scots Porage Oats, Colman's mustard, Cadbury's foods, Mellow Birds coffee, Dunhill pipe tobacco, Guinness, and Bulmer's Cider.

GENEALOGY AND FAMILY HISTORY

As the interest in family history and roots grows world-wide, more and more people are turning to Frith's photographs of Great Britain for images of the towns, villages and streets where their ancestors lived; and, of course, photographs of the churches and chapels where their ancestors were christened, married and buried are an essential part of every genealogy tree and family album.

FRITH PRODUCTS

All Frith photographs are available Framed or just as Mounted Prints and unmounted versions. These may be ordered from the address below. Other products available are - Calendars, Jigsaws, Canvas Prints, Mugs, Tea Towels, Tableware and local and prestige books.

THE INTERNET

Over several hundred thousand Frith photographs can be viewed and purchased on the internet through the Frith websites!

For more detailed information on Frith products, look at **www.francisfrith.com**

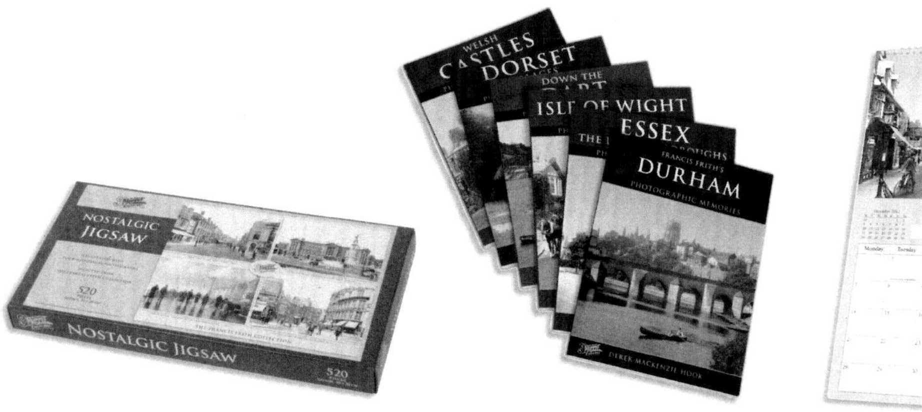
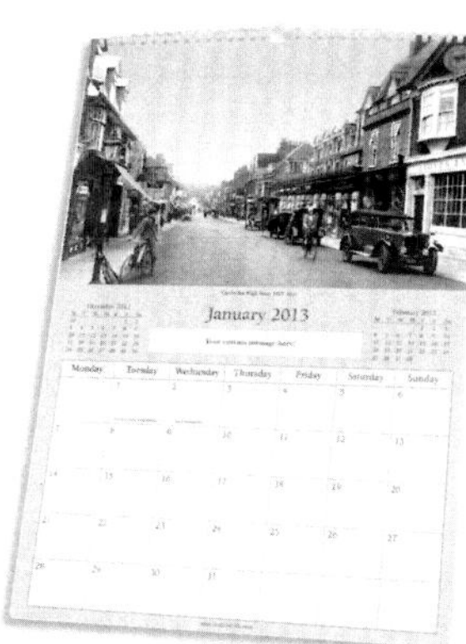

See the complete list of Frith Books at: www.francisfrith.com
This web site is regularly updated with the latest list of publications from The Francis Frith Collection. If you wish to buy books relating to another part of the country that your local bookshop does not stock, you may purchase on-line.

For further information, trade, or author enquiries please contact us at the address below:
The Francis Frith Collection, Unit 19 Kingsmead Business Park, Gillingham, Dorset SP8 5FB.
Tel: +44 (0)1722 716 376   Email: sales@francisfrith.co.uk

See Frith products on the internet at www.francisfrith.com

FREE PRINT OF YOUR CHOICE
CHOOSE A PHOTOGRAPH FROM THIS BOOK

+ POSTAGE

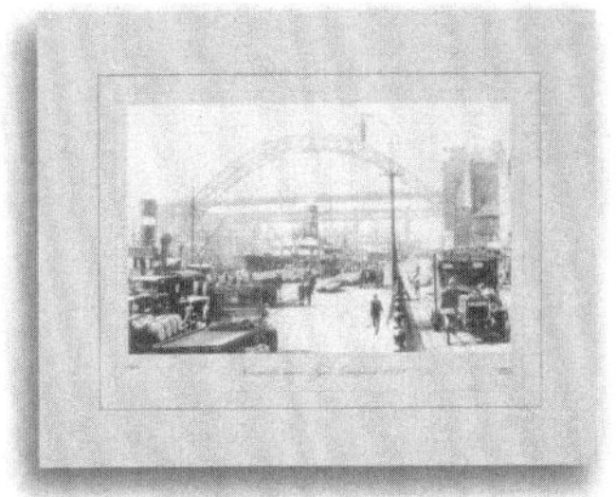

Mounted Print

Overall size 14 x 11 inches (355 x 280mm)

TO RECEIVE YOUR FREE PRINT

Choose any Frith photograph in this book

Simply complete the Voucher opposite and
return it with your payment (to cover postage
and handling) and we will print the photograph
of your choice in SEPIA (size 11 x 8 inches) and
supply it in a cream mount ready to frame
(overall size 14 x 11 inches).

Order additional Mounted Prints
at HALF PRICE - £19.00 each (normally £38.00)

If you would like to order more Frith prints
from this book, possibly as gifts for friends and
family, you can buy them at half price (with no
additional postage costs).

Have your Mounted Prints framed

For an extra £20.00 per print you can have your
mounted print(s) framed in an elegant polished
wood and gilt moulding, overall size
16 x 13 inches (no additional postage required).

IMPORTANT!

❶ Please note: aerial photographs and photographs
with a reference number starting with a "Z" are not Frith
photographs and cannot be supplied under this offer.

❷ Offer valid for delivery to one UK address only.

❸ These special prices are only available if you use this
form to order. You must use the ORIGINAL VOUCHER on
this page (no copies permitted). We can only despatch
to one UK address.

❹ This offer cannot be combined with any other offer.

As a customer your name & address will be stored by Frith but not sold or rented
to third parties. Your data will be used for the purpose of this promotion only.

Send completed Voucher form to:

The Francis Frith Collection,
1 Chilmark Estate House, Chilmark,
Salisbury, Wiltshire SP3 5DU

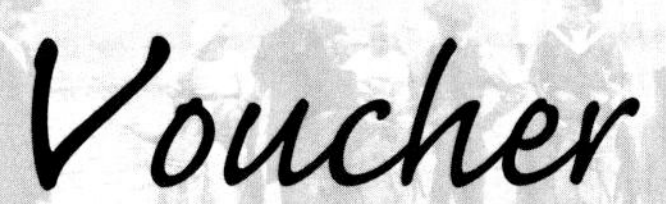

Voucher for *FREE* and Reduced Price Frith Prints

Please do not photocopy this voucher. Only the original is valid,
so please fill it in, cut it out and return it to us with your order.

Picture ref no	Page no	Qty	Mounted @ £19.00	Framed + £20.00	Total Cost £
		1	Free of charge*	£	£
			£19.00	£	£
			£19.00	£	£
			£19.00	£	£
			£19.00	£	£
			£19.00	£	£

Please allow 28 days for delivery.
Offer available to one UK address only

* Post & handling	£3.80
Total Order Cost	£

Title of this book . . . .

I enclose a cheque/postal order for £ . . . .
made payable to 'Heritage Resource Management Ltd'

OR please debit my Mastercard / Visa / Maestro card,
details below

Card Number:

Issue No (Maestro only):   Valid from (Maestro):

Card Security Number: Expires:

Signature:

Name Mr/Mrs/Ms . . . .

Address . . . .

. . . .

. . . .

. . . . Postcode . . . .

Daytime Tel No . . . .

Email . . . .

Valid to 31/12/26

FF028683

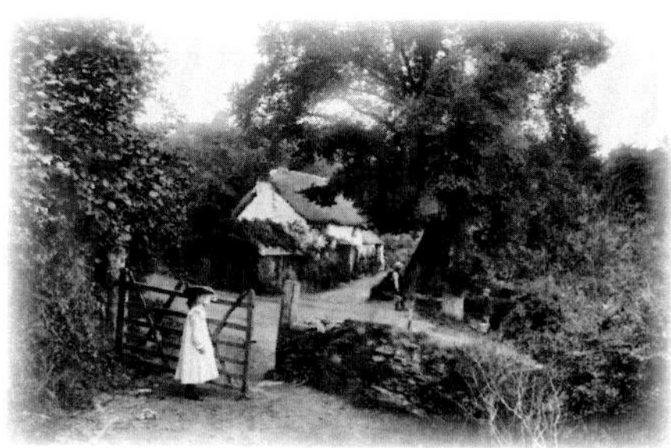

Can you help us with information about any of the Frith photographs in this book?

We are gradually compiling an historical record for each of the photographs in the Frith archive. It is always fascinating to find out the names of the people shown in the pictures, as well as insights into the shops, buildings and other features depicted.

If you recognize anyone in the photographs in this book, or if you have information not already included in the author's caption, do let us know. We would love to hear from you, and will try to publish it in future books or articles.

An Invitation from The Francis Frith Collection to Share Your Memories

The 'Share Your Memories' feature of our website allows members of the public to add personal memories relating to the places featured in our photographs, or comment on others already added. Seeing a place from your past can rekindle forgotten or long held memories. Why not visit the website, find photographs of places you know well and add YOUR story for others to read and enjoy? We would love to hear from you!

www.francisfrith.com/memories

Our production team

Frith books are produced by a small dedicated team at offices near Salisbury. Most have worked with the Frith Collection for many years. All have in common one quality: they have a passion for the Frith Collection.

Frith Books and Gifts

We have a wide range of books and gifts available on our website utilising our photographic archive, many of which can be individually personalised.

www.francisfrith.com